Letters Written during the Late Voyage of Discovery in the Western Arctic Sea

Anonymous

CAMBRIDGE
UNIVERSITY PRESS

University Printing House, Cambridge, CB2 8BS, United Kingdom

Cambridge University Press is part of the University of Cambridge.
It furthers the University's mission by disseminating knowledge in the pursuit of
education, learning and research at the highest international levels of excellence.

www.cambridge.org
Information on this title: www.cambridge.org/9781108073400

© in this compilation Cambridge University Press 2014

This edition first published 1821
This digitally printed version 2014

ISBN 978-1-108-07340-0 Paperback

This book reproduces the text of the original edition. The content and language reflect
the beliefs, practices and terminology of their time, and have not been updated.

Cambridge University Press wishes to make clear that the book, unless originally published
by Cambridge, is not being republished by, in association or collaboration with,
or with the endorsement or approval of, the original publisher or its successors in title.

CAMBRIDGE LIBRARY COLLECTION

Books of enduring scholarly value

Polar Exploration

This series includes accounts, by eye-witnesses and contemporaries, of early expeditions to the Arctic and the Antarctic. Huge resources were invested in such endeavours, particularly the search for the North-West Passage, which, if successful, promised enormous strategic and commercial rewards. Cartographers and scientists travelled with many of the expeditions, and their work made important contributions to earth sciences, climatology, botany and zoology. They also brought back anthropological information about the indigenous peoples of the Arctic region and the southern fringes of the American continent. The series further includes dramatic and poignant accounts of the harsh realities of working in extreme conditions and utter isolation in bygone centuries.

Letters Written during the Late Voyage of Discovery in the Western Arctic Sea

Sir Edward Parry (1790–1855) wrote accounts of his three Arctic expeditions, which have also been reissued in this series. This book takes the form of letters written to a sibling by an anonymous member of the crew on Parry's 1819–20 voyage. It was brought out in 1821 by the enterprising publisher Richard Phillips ahead of any other narrative, as all accounts and journals had first to be handed to the Admiralty Board for the extraction of any important details. It seems likely that the work, which is carefully constructed and elegant in style, was elaborated either from notes or from a genuine series of letters, to get round the restriction on publication. This is a fascinating narrative, full of striking details, such as entertainments on board to help morale, the reappearance of the sun at the end of the Arctic winter, and the sight of the aurora borealis.

Cambridge University Press has long been a pioneer in the reissuing of out-of-print titles from its own backlist, producing digital reprints of books that are still sought after by scholars and students but could not be reprinted economically using traditional technology. The Cambridge Library Collection extends this activity to a wider range of books which are still of importance to researchers and professionals, either for the source material they contain, or as landmarks in the history of their academic discipline.

Drawing from the world-renowned collections in the Cambridge University Library and other partner libraries, and guided by the advice of experts in each subject area, Cambridge University Press is using state-of-the-art scanning machines in its own Printing House to capture the content of each book selected for inclusion. The files are processed to give a consistently clear, crisp image, and the books finished to the high quality standard for which the Press is recognised around the world. The latest print-on-demand technology ensures that the books will remain available indefinitely, and that orders for single or multiple copies can quickly be supplied.

The Cambridge Library Collection brings back to life books of enduring scholarly value (including out-of-copyright works originally issued by other publishers) across a wide range of disciplines in the humanities and social sciences and in science and technology.

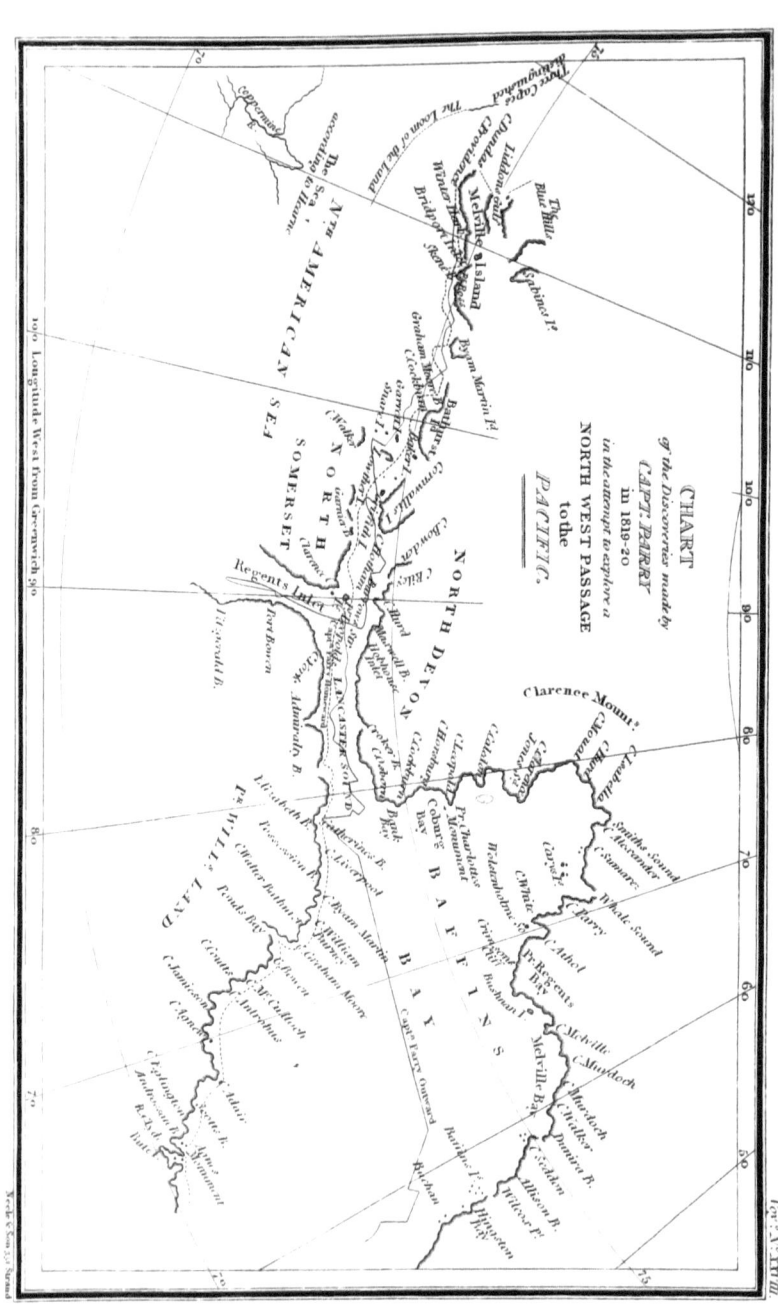

LETTERS

WRITTEN DURING

THE LATE

VOYAGE OF DISCOVERY

IN THE

𝔚𝔢𝔰𝔱𝔢𝔯𝔫 𝔄𝔯𝔠𝔱𝔦𝔠 𝔖𝔢𝔞.

BY AN OFFICER OF THE EXPEDITION.

LONDON:

PRINTED FOR SIR RICHARD PHILLIPS AND Co.

BRIDE-COURT, BRIDGE STREET.

1821.

G. SIDNEY, Printer,
Northumberland Street, Strand.

PREFACE.

THE Public are probably aware that, agreeably to a regulation of the Admiralty, all Journals of Voyages of Discovery, kept by Officers or others, are required to be temporarily surrendered for the use of that Board: hence it has happened, that we have been unable till now to submit to our Readers full details of Captain Parry's last Voyage.

We have, however, been so fortunate as to recompense them for the delay, by introducing to their perusal one of the most consistent, intelligent, and interesting Accounts, that have yet appeared of a Voyage which has excited so great a degree of Public Interest.

In making this observation, we have, however, no intention to depreciate the Classical Production of Captain PARRY, or the accurate and modest Journal of Mr. FISHER, whose works would have sufficed to record the Incidents of this Voyage, if it had not been our duty, as Journalists in this branch of Literature, to submit the best account which we are able to obtain.

In this task we have succeeded to our own wishes, and we hope we have performed our Duty to the satisfaction of our Readers on this, as we have done on every other occasion.

As the appearance of this Number has been unavoidably delayed beyond our usual period of Publication, we have yielded to the solicitation of many Country Subscribers, and resolved to Publish this, and every future Number, on the FIRST DAY *of the Month, with the other Journals and Magazines, instead of the* FIFTEENTH *as heretofore. This will accord better with the routine of Periodical Publications, and confer a freshness on our Numbers more agreeable to those Subscribers who have hitherto been unable to obtain them till the commencement of the Month.*

LETTERS

WRITTEN DURING

THE LATE

VOYAGE OF DISCOVERY,

IN THE

Western Arctic Sea.

LETTER I.

DEAR BROTHER,   11*th May*, 1819.

AGREEABLY to my promise, I now begin my account of our proceedings and our observations, in the important expedition on which we have embarked. You were never at sea, but you showed always a particular taste for descriptions of voyages to distant or unknown, or little known parts of the world. The enterprise in which we are engaged will, certainly, if we have any success, carry us into scenes presenting objects of novelty at least, if not of importance and value. We may, I trust, if we do no more, satisfy ourselves, convince perhaps our countrymen at home, and navigators of all nations, that a practicable communication by sea, round the northern coasts of North America, is not to be attained. To ascertain even this point is an object of no small importance. It will abundantly justify the expense to the nation, and the dangers to the persons employed in the research.

As my letters, if ever they arrive in Marybone, (and when and how they are to be forwarded I know not,) will soon pass from your hands into those of many kind friends, equally strangers with yourself to sea affairs and sea language, I will endeavour to steer clear if possible of obscurity arising from such peculiarities. Being, however, formed on my regular Journal, nautical operations and incidents cannot always be expressed without nautical terms and phrases.

A sea-journal is the production of every day; but however important the occurrences and transactions of every day are to the seaman, to the landsman they often appear dull and uninteresting. You will not, therefore expect me to transmit to you details, in which you would feel little concern, and the value of which you could not often comprehend. With respect, however, to the time when, and the place where such and such incidents or operations occurred, I shall be careful to give you correct notices. For you must know that, although continually, in some sense, the sport of waves and winds, no human being leads a life so regular and methodical as the mariner.

The ships appointed for this expedition, to search for a northwest passage from the Atlantic ocean to the Pacific, are the Hecla, so named after the famous burning mountain in Iceland, in allusion to her destination as a bomb-vessel, to discharge inflamed substances on an enemy. She was built, I hear, in 1815; and by her peculiar shape and capaciousness, (nearly four hundred tons,) is well adapted to receive the large stock of necessaries of all kinds, for the ship's company, during a voyage of probably long duration. The other ship, the Griper, is a gun-brig, but materially improved by raising her, to enlarge her stowage. Still she has not enough of accommodation for all the stores, &c. requisite for the people on board; but must depend for some supplies on the Hecla. The whole ship's company of the Hecla consists of fifty-eight persons, officers, seamen, and marines; that of the Griper of thirty-six. Both vessels have received every additional strengthening which wood and iron can give them, particularly on the bows, to resist the shock in making their way through the ice. In the inside they are fitted up in the most comfortable manner, for all on board; and every article of clothing, food, medicines, &c., which can be foreseen to be requisite, has been plentifully supplied. Nor have such things been omitted as may serve to conciliate the natives of the countries we may visit. Nothing omitted, nothing in fact has been refused by the Lords of the Admiralty which was supposed, or suggested to be useful in promoting the safety, the health, and the comfort of all persons employed in the expedition. With the view of improving the nautical and geographical knowledge of those quarters of the globe through which we may pass, a very complete assortment of instruments of the best construction are put on board, together with every implement requisite for the accurate construction of charts and maps.

Both ships were ready to fall down the river from Deptford early in April; but they were detained by contrary winds till the beginning of this month, when the season seemed to be sufficiently advanced for our setting off. On Tuesday morning, therefore, the 4th inst., the Hecla was towed by a steam-vessel down to Northfleet, a little above Gravesend, and the Griper followed at night. Thus it has happened that the present expedition sails just a month later than the former, of 1818, in the ships Isabella and Alexander. The commander of the Hecla, and of the expedition, is Lieutenant William Edward Parry: the Griper is commanded by Lieutenant Matthew Liddon. The Admiralty having granted to all those officers, seamen, and marines, who should be employed in the expedition, double the ordinary pay of the Navy, the vessels were soon furnished with the full number of the best seamen. It is not a little encouraging also to observe that, with a few exceptions, every man who served in the former enterprise, has volunteered his services in the present.

On Thursday the 6th we received on board, from the arsenal of Woolwich, our ordnance stores; and on Friday the powder. To obviate as much as might be done the effects of the iron guns on the quarter-deck, upon the compass, they have been removed, and their place supplied by brass.

Saturday 8*th.*—Worked down to the Nore off Sheerness and received on board the various instruments for making observations for astronomical, nautical, geographical, and meteorological purposes. Several of the officers have also carried out instruments of their own property. As far therefore as those indispensable assistants can be procured, our expedition promises all reasonable success.

Monday 10*th.*—The seamen and marines have received the wages due to them since they entered, with an advance of three months' pay; that they may provide various articles of clothing, and other necessaries for the voyage, agreeably to a list furnished by the officers on board. Some bullocks, beer, and the proper stock of water being brought off, all was ready for getting under weigh. This operation took place this morning at ten o'clock, and before sun-set we had got out of the difficult passes between the banks in the mouth of the Thames.

Of my feelings on this occasion, then, it will be just as easy for you to form, as for me to convey any exact idea. This is not the first time of my leaving England on a long voyage; but such is the nature of the present expedition, such are its purposes, such the accidents to which we must be prepared to expose ourselves, that it is impossible for me to suppress certain apprehensions and forebodings, to which I have hitherto been a stranger.—But as the French say *le vin est tiré il faut le boire.* Duty, respect and affection to all at home, and be assured.

&c. &c.

LETTER II.

MY DEAR BROTHER, *At sea, Wednesday, 26th May, 1819.*

You received, I hope, my long epistle of the 11th, which, by good fortune, was sent on shore from Yarmouth roads, by a boat belonging to H. M.'s ship Wye, on Saturday the 15th. Since then we have lost sight of every part and appendage of the British isles; and I now write to you from the great Atlantic ocean, from a spot due south from the centre of Iceland, and due west from the centre of Scotland. If you will turn up your Atlas to such a position at the intersection of the meridian of $20°\ 45'$ west from Greenwich, and the parallel of $57°\ 3'$ North Latitude, you will then be able to give my mother and Mary some idea of the spot where, in imagination, I am as busy in conversing with you all as if I were seated beside you.

My last letter closed at the commencement of our voyage, since which we have been constantly under weigh, with the exception of short interruptions on the coast of Norfolk, in Yarmouth roads. The narrow passages between the sand banks and the land, and between one another, afford the only shelter for shipping in easterly winds to be found on the English coast of the German ocean. For that reason these passes are much resorted to; but for the same reason shipwrecks are there by no means rare. The Yarmouth boatmen are however of great service to the people on board, by their courage and skill in rescuing them from the wrecks. Just such an account as this you have heard me give of the advantages and dangers of the Godwin Sands and the Downs, and of the boatmen of Deal.

Before we arrived off Yarmouth we discovered that the Griper was in general no match for the Hecla in sailing, excepting on a wind; it became necessary, therefore, on several occasions, for the Hecla either to take her in tow, or to lie to, to wait for her getting up.

The voyage properly began at noon on Tuesday the 11th, when we left the river, and commenced our experiments and observations on the state of the weather and on the temperature of the air and the sea. On that day the thermometer in the shade stood at sixty-two degrees; the temperature of the surface of the sea was 57 degrees, and the barometer was at 30·19 inches. Early on the morning of Friday the 14th, while turning up to the northward, the wind being contrary and the sea rough, the Hecla touched on the east end of Sheringham shoal, occasioned by the pilot carrying the ship too far to the westward. But the alarm was soon over, and no bad consequences followed from the accident.

It is common, you know, for land folks to charge us seamen with not being over attentive to our religious duties. It ought to be considered, however, that winds and waves know no distinction of days and times. The operations on ship-board must, of necessity, be performed at all hours, and it is not surprising, that by habit the sailor should become less regular in his devotions than persons on land, whose time is wholly at their own disposal. To show you, however, that the charge against us is not always well founded, you must know, that on Sunday the 16th, divine service was performed on board both ships, and attended by every officer and man who could be spared from the indispensable duties on deck.

Monday the 17th, being off the coast of Yorkshire, distant from twelve to fourteen miles, we discharged our pilot from the Thames. He carried back with him a number of letters, among which, were a few lines from me, just to say that we were then all well. In the afternoon of Tuesday the 18th, we had a distant view of the mountains beyond Aberdeen, on the north coast of Scotland; and, on the following afternoon, we came in sight of Fair Island, situated between the Orkney and the Shetland isles. Since Sunday morning the wind has been favourable, and the weather pleasant. Several flocks of divers, a bird frequently seen in Davis's Strait and in Baffin's Bay, have come near us; also that kind, called by seamen the puffin. The people caught a number of excellent cod and coal-fish off Fair Island.

On *Thursday* the 20th, we were detained by calms; but, in the evening, the wind springing up, carried us round the north point of the Orkney isles, distant from two to three miles. From what I have learned on board, the appearance of these islands may be considered as a sort of intermediate step between the favoured land which we have left, and the·dreary regions to which we are bound. In the morning we passed a Danish whaler, on her voyage to Davis's Strait; but she steered a course more to the northward than we did. In the morning of *Friday* the 21st, we lost sight of the Orkneys, and, in the evening, we descried Rona and Bara, two small islands, the former inhabited, situated a little to the northward of the parallel of 59°, and the most northern of the western islands of Scotland. In the neighbourhood of these isles we saw vast numbers of sea-fowl of different kinds, which resort thither and to other remote islands in that quarter, situated in the open sea, where proper food is found in abundance. I mentioned that the Danish ship kept a course to the northward of us: but we steered according to the opinion of the most skilful captains in the whale trade, who cross the Atlantic in or a little to the southward of lat. 58°.

Saturday 22d.—You have occasionally read in the newspapers of sealed bottles being met with at sea, or driven ashore in several parts, containing notes of the time and place of their being thrown into the sea. One was thrown overboard to day from the Hecla, in which was a paper, containing a request, in various languages, that whoever should find it would transmit it to the Admiralty, in London, mentioning where and when it was found. This is done every day that the ships are under weigh. The principal object of this custom is, that, by comparing the times and places of the throwing out and the picking up of the bottles, if found at sea, or immediately after they are driven ashore, a calculation may be made of the direction and the motion of the currents of the water by which the bottles have been conveyed along. A bottle of this kind, I am informed, was found on the north-west coast of Ireland, which had been thrown overboard in the former voyage to Baffin's Bay. It had been ten months in the sea, and must have been carried by the currents upwards of a thousand miles in that time. The chance of conveying, by the same means, to all concerned, intelligence of the state of a ship, is, of itself, sufficient to engage those on board to its adoption.

Monday 24th.—This day we came in sight of Rockall, a single mass of rock springing up in the midst of the ocean, about fifty leagues, that is, one hundred and fifty marine or geographical miles, equal to a hundred and seventy-two English miles from the nearest land, the western isles of Scotland. It is situated in north latitude $57° 39\frac{1}{2}$, and west longitude $13° 31$ from Greenwich. Imagine to yourself the perfection to which instruments for the use of seamen must be now brought, when the position of an object so diminutive can be ascertained with such accuracy, that they can navigate the surrounding seas without fear of running against Rockall at any hour, day or night. At a distance it might, from its shape or colour, be mistaken for a ship under sail. When we had got about thirty miles west from Rockall, we found the depth of water to be only one hundred and forty fathoms. The temperature of the air, in the evening, was $50°$, while that of the sea, at the surface, was $49°\frac{1}{2}$, and, at the bottom $47°\frac{3}{4}$.

Before we left England I had, as you know, taken some pains to collect the most authentic notices relative to the history of the regions we were destined to explore. The result of my inquiries I had no time to communicate to you; but, having employed some spare time in committing it to paper since we have been at sea, it shall be the subject of my next letter.

Adieu,

Your, &c. &c.

LETTER III.

My dear Brother,   At Sea, 30th May, 1819.

I now send to you, as I promised, some heads relative to the early state of these northern regions, among which you will find several things which will be new to you, and which may furnish subjects for conversation in the happy circle in ——— street. Chronology and geography are described as the two eyes of history : both shall therefore be kept open in what I have to state.

About A.D. 500, according to the Icelandic historians, some Irish monks, whether by accident or by design, arrived in Iceland ; wafted over the northern ocean in fourteen days, in their coracles, or wicker boats, covered with hides. Books in the ancient Irish language, bells, &c. were found in the island, on the arrival of the earliest settlers from Norway.

A.D. 890.—Harold Harfagur, the first king of all Norway, having conquered all his rivals, or usurped the chief power, compelled many bodies of the people to quit their native land. Resorting to their ships, they formed settlements in the most remote parts of the North. Of those colonies, the most distinguished was established in Iceland, which had been accidentally visited in 861, and occupied in 878. This colony, if we except those of the ancient Greeks, is the only colony in the world, prior to the comparatively late settlements of Europeans in America, of which a regular account has been preserved from its commencement to the present time.

Towards the beginning of the tenth century, the Icelanders established a colony in Greenland, which increased and prospered for nearly four hundred years. Then the intercourse between that region and the rest of the world was interrupted, by the increasing severity of the climate, and the unfortunate colonists were no more heard of. Navigators of the present age, who depend on the assistance of the compass and quadrant ; who are furnished with arithmetical and mathematical tables, calculated with the greatest nicety ; must be astonished at the daring spirit of these adventurous sons of the Northern Seas, who were unquestionably destitute of those aids.

It is related by an Icelandic historian, that when Flok, a famous Norwegian navigator, was preparing to set out from the isles of Hialtland, now called Zetland or Shetland, on the north of Scotland, on a voyage to Iceland, then named Gardarsholm, he took on board as guides, *some crows, because the mariner's com-*

pass was not at that time in use. When he thought he had made a good part of his voyage, Flok threw up in the air one of his crows, which seeing land astern, or behind, flew back to it. Concluding the land he had left to be the nearest in sight (but perhaps he mistook the Feroe for the Shetland Isles on this occasion) he held on his course for some time, and then sent off another crow, which seeing land a-head, or before the ship, drove forward towards it. Following his sagacious guide, Flok arrived at the east end of Iceland. Such were the simple means employed in those days by the intrepid men of the North, to keep their reckoning, and steer their course over the ocean. A similar mode is said to have been practised by the people of Ceylon in early times: but what a difference between the gentle waters of India, and the tempestuous billows of the North Atlantic!

In the close of the 9th century, our renowned king Alfred was perhaps the first Briton to enlarge the science of geography. From Ohther and Wulfstan he received ample information respecting the Baltic sea and the Northern extremities of Europe. But the knowledge collected by Alfred seems to have been lost; for even in the 16th century, Norway, Greenland, and Newfoundland, (or the land of cod-fish) are described as forming one continued country. And it was not till 1553, that Chancellor traced out the northern passage to Russia, of which he has always been described as the original discoverer. It is nevertheless certain that Ohther the Norwegian sailed round the North cape of Lapland and made his way into the White Sea of Archangel, then called Quen Sea, of which the modern name is only a translation. From Ohther, Alfred learned that the northern people caught whales and seals, and also what he calls horse-whales. Of the skins were made ropes, and the teeth of the latter animals were highly valued. From this account the horse-whale seems to have been the animal now called the walrus, or sea-horse, whose tusks are ivory. The whales are stated to be in length forty-eight or fifty Norwegian ells, or from seventy-two to seventy-five feet. So numerous were they on the coast of Norway, that Ohther, with the help of five men, was able, we are told, to kill sixty in two or three days.

In the last year of the tenth century, or in the first year of the eleventh, the adventurous spirit of the Icelanders carried them to a distant country, situated to the south-west of Greenland. There, in the shortest day, the sun was for eight hours above the horizon. Here, then, is a question for you to solve; for you are astronomer enough to do it. You will find that this happens about the parallel of 49 degrees of north latitude. The country being much wooded, was, therefore, named Merkland; but grapes having been discovered growing spontaneously in it, the name was changed to Winland. The rivers abounded with fish, particularly with salmon. It was not until their third voyage to this country that the Icelanders met with any original inhabitants, who appeared a diminutive race. They had boats covered with hides, and used bows and arrows in battle. After a contest the natives were reconciled to the Icelanders and traded with them, exchanging furs for other articles of utility or fancy. Several vessels from Iceland for this *new-found-land* carried thither families to form a permanent settlement, which it would appear subsisted for above a century for a bishop went thither from the colony in Greenland, in the year 1121. Of this settlement no certain accounts, nor of its connexion with Iceland, are afterwards discovered in history If it be true, as has been reported, that in the interior of Newfoundland a tribe exists, different from the Americans called Esquimaux, they may, perhaps, be the descendants of the Icelanders. That they should however retain any tradition of their original story, or any vestige of the Icelandic tongue, in their state of barbarism, cannot well be expected.

The discoverer of Winland is said to have been Biorn, the son of Heriolf, and the first ship purp sely fitted out for the new country from Iceland was commanded by Lief, the son of Erick.

About 1360, Nicolas of Lynne, an English friar, and a good astronomer, is said to have made a voyage to the northern polar regions, and to have repeated the voyage for five times afterwards. Of his discoveries he presented an account to Edward III. but of the truth of the story we may be allowed to doubt. About the same period, according to the account of the voyage of the Venetian Zeno, as explained by Forster, some fishermen of Orkney were driven by stress of weather to an island in the west, called Estotiland. The inhabitants traded with those of Greenland, and to what we now call America. They were ignorant of the compass, but soon learned its use from the Orkneymen. This island may perhaps have been the Winland of the Icelanders, or the Newfoundland of later times.

If these incidents be really true, it will be evident that the new world, the northern part of it at least, was visited by European navigators, long prior to the voyage of the illustrious Colon, or Columbus, in 1492. Nothing derogatory from his well-earned fame can however hence be inferred; for his discoveries were the fruit of long and profound scientific research.

Best wishes at home, &c. &c.

LETTER IV

Dear Brother, *At Sea, 23d June,* 1819.
My last journal-letter brought down our proceedings to the 26th of last month, since which day the weather has been variable, but my health and spirits have been invariably good. It is Dr. Johnson, I think, who speaks of a worthy gentleman who, from an early point of life, kept a regular record of the state and changes of the weather. At the age of threescore and ten or so, the result of his observations was, that the weather was changeable. This notable discovery might satisfy the person who, in cold, wet, or boisterous seasons, could resort to his warm room and comfortable fire : but for people in our situation and our profession, something more determinate is not only desirable but absolutely necessary, to enable us to prepare and provide against whatever change in the atmosphere may occur. The bad sailing of the Griper when before the wind, precisely the time when we ought to push forward as much as possible, is a most unfortunate quality; which her good sailing upon a wind will not, I fear, be sufficient to compensate. When the wind is quite fair, therefore, the Hecla must either take her in tow, or lie to for her, from time to time, till she make up with her consort. How much this circumstance, and in such a voyage too, mortifies the companies of both ships, it is impossible for you as a landsman to imagine.

The most remarkable occurrences, since my letter of the 26th past, are the unexpected discovery of land on Tuesday the 15th of this month, at a great distance to the northward, and the falling in with floating ice for the first time yesterday. When land was observed we were on the meridian of west longitude $42° 57'$, which is that of Cape Farewell, the southernmost point of the Greenland coast. But as that cape lies in north latitude $59° 37\frac{1}{2}'$, and we were in $57° 26'$, our distance coinciding with the difference of latitude was about $2° 12'$ or 132 miles, or 44 leagues. Here, squire, is another opportunity for applying your skill in calculation. The eye of the observer being raised twenty feet above the surface of the sea, and the summit of Cape Farewell being visible in the horizon at the distance of 132 nautical, not English miles, what must be the height of the mountains at the Cape ; all regard to the refraction of light and the irregular curvature of the earth being laid out of the computation?

The ice we met with yesterday is what, in the language of Greenland fishers, is called stream ice, or a number of loose broken pieces so far asunder as to allow a ship to make way among them. Besides these detached masses, we saw also a number of icebergs or icehills afloat. These objects were interesting to a stranger like me; but I am advised to reserve my wonder for masses of a very different description, to be encountered as we proceed farther to the northward. Wonder is not, as you may imagine, the only feeling excited by the view of an iceberg and of the ice in general. It is impossible to avoid foreboding what must be the situation of a ship encompassed by such tremendous bodies of ice, whether in motion or firmly adhering together. In speaking of the view of Cape Farewell, I should have noticed that our view of that remote head-land was chiefly owing to the peculiar clearness of the atmosphere, which is always produced by its humidity immediately after, and some times immediately before, rain. I ought also to have mentioned that, on the 30th and 31st past, we ran over the spot called in some charts the sunken land of Buss, on which the water is said to be far less deep than is generally found in that part of the Atlantic. With various lengths of line, however, up to 160 and 170 fathoms, no bottom could be found. Hence the existence of a bank in that position may well be doubted.

On Tuesday the first of this month the weather, notwithstanding the advance of the summer, was colder and more uncomfortable than at any time since we put to sea, from the thick rain and fog; the latter preparing us for what we must expect as we get on into Davis's Strait and Baffin's Bay. You good people of London complain in doleful strain of a fog in the streets: but you have at least the houses on each hand to guide you on your way from Charing Cross to Change Alley. Think, however, what must be our embarrassment in the wide ocean, incumbered with hills and plains of ice in our course and on every side, with the compass alone to point out our direction, when we cannot see twice the ship's length before us. During that and the following day several birds, of land as well as sea, were hovering about us. The snow-bunting in particular must have come all the way from the Greenland coast, nearly 400 miles; for the wind came from that quarter. The arctic-gull, so called from its usually resorting to the northern regions, appeared also for the first time. The wind drawing much to the north-west we were obliged to stand to the southward on the first of the month, and continued so to do to the fourth, when the gale, which had for two days been very boisterous, allowed us to steer towards the north-west. On the first we were in latitude by observation at noon 58° 7': but on the fourth we had been driven southward nearly to 55° that is to the parallel of the north of England. In longitude we had gained only from 33° 31' to 35° 22': and, indeed, it may be said that up to the 15th, this month has been in general tempestuous; and, which is worst of all, the wind has been always against us.

On *Wednesday* the 2d, the gale blew very hard; and we had, in the afternoon, a visit from those ill-omened birds, as the seamen reckon them, the stormy peterel, commonly called Mother Carey's chickens. But, if they are supposed to appear about a ship some hours before a storm come on, they, at the same time, give the seamen so much warning to put his vessel in proper trim to receive and weather it. Whether they possess any peculiar sense or instinct, by which they discover the approach of a tempest, before it be sensible to human beings, it is not for me to say; but their collecting round or under the lee of a ship, seems clearly for the sake of shelter and protection from the violence of the winds, which they are unable to resist. This was evident from the position the birds always chose under the lee-quarter of the ship; and, if at any time they let her get a-head of them for thirty or forty yards, they quickly return to that part of the ship where they had been before. Although the gale abated sensibly in the evening of the 3d, the peterels kept their station under the ship until its violence was quite gone. Friday the 4th, being the anniversary of our venerable sovereign's birth-day, it was celebrated on board both vessels, with every mark of respect which our circumstances allowed. To the men an extra quantity of spirits was distributed for grog, or, as they express it, the main brace was spliced: and the weather being now calm and fine, they closed their festivity with a merry dance on deck.

This easy weather did not, however, last long, for on the 7th and 8th we had severe gales from the westward, which raised up a heavy sea; and, altogether, the weather was much against our progress. During this time we saw a number of whales called finners, because they have on the back a fin, which often rises above the surface when the body is quite under water. This species is of about the same length with the common black whale of Greenland; that is, fifty or sixty feet long, but not so thick. Being less easy to kill than the other, and affording less oil, the finners are not particularly sought after by the fishers. Various other animals, both fish and birds, the ordinary inhabitants of the arctic regions, also appeared at the same time.

On *Sunday* the 13*th,* the weather being favourable, by observations of the sun's position, we ascertained the variation of the compass, that is, the deviation of the magnetic needle from the true meridian. This deviation, as it had been expected, turned out to be very considerable, increasing regularly ever since we left Britain. On the 19th we observed a great change in the colour of the sea, since we got among the ice, having assumed a dark brown tint, instead of the fine blue of the Atlantic. This tinge was, doubtless, produced by the dissolution of the ice, over and round which were numbers of the little divers, or rotges; from which circumstance they are generally called ice-birds. The ice had a very sensible effect on the temperature of the sea. On the 19th we observed the variation of the magnetic needle to be 48°3 westerly; but in these high latitudes, especially approaching the supposed north magnetic pole of the earth, the ascertainment of the variation on board ship is an operation of no small difficulty. In the evening we had a view of the west coast of Greenland, about Cape Desolation, the ships being at noon in north lat. 59° 48′, and in west long. 48° 2′. Here we discovered a current setting towards S.W at the rate of about six miles in the twenty-four hours.

Sunday 20th.—The Greenland coast again came in sight, distant twelve or thirteen leagues to the eastward The water still of a dirty tinge, although no bottom was found at a depth of one hundred and forty fathoms. The breeze from the eastward, which came on in the evening of the 19th, carried us in a W.N.W direction through the ice, so broken, however, as to admit the ships to make way, or what the fishers call sailing ice. In this open sea we proceeded till noon of this day, when we discovered several icebergs in the line of our course towards the north-west; having now arrived in latitude 62° 43′, and longitude 61° 33′. Coming in the evening near one of those masses of ice, we found the depth of water to be about two hundred fathoms; while the berg, which did not appear to be fast to the ground, rose from fifty to sixty feet above the water.

Having conducted you fairly into the frozen waters of the entrance into Davis's Strait, I must lay down my pen until another opportunity presents itself of communicating my remarks on scenes in which novelty and interest must be combined.

Best regards at home, &c.

LETTER V.

Davis's Strait, 31st July, 1819.

DEAR BROTHER,

I RESUME my pen to inform you, that at last we have arrived at the entrance of Sir James Lancaster's Sound, on which so much has been said, since the return of the ships employed in the expedition of last year. At this point may be properly said to begin our exploratory voyage; for, hitherto, we have been engaged in tracts of sea, more or less frequented by whalers for many years past. From our proper entrance into the ice, which occupies the middle of this strait, we worked to the northward, in the hope of discovering a passage in it to gain the American shore. This, however, was impracticable, until we reached nearly to the latitude of the south point of Lancaster Sound, where, by means of the greatest perseverance, in spite of every obstacle, we happily effected our course. Then, for the first time, did I descry any part of the transatlantic world.—But, to be more particular : my last letter, of the 23d June, would inform you of our arrival on the border of the central ice of Davis's Strait, on Wednesday the 23d of last month. In the morning of the 24th, which was thick and hazy, we found our progress interrupted by a range of icebergs, extending from S. to N. for several miles, and the intervals between them filled with extended stretches of floating, but continuous ice, quite obstructing all passage. That no effort, however, might be spared, to force our course to the westward, we entered a short way into the ice, and, in the morning of the 24th, the boats were sent a-head to tow the ships; for the wind, though from the eastward, was very feeble. In the afternoon, unfortunately, a breeze sprung up from the westward, which not only opposed our course, but brought soon upon us the floating ice from that quarter, and so quickly, that the boats could hardly be got in, when both vessels were completely beset, as it is termed, or blocked in, for a breadth of three miles at least, to the eastward, where only any clear sea could be seen.

On *Sunday* the 27*th*, the wind blew hard from the northward, by which the ice, and consequently the ships, were drifted nearly fourteen miles to the southward of the point where they were beset. This drift was discovered by observing our latitude by the sun's meridian altitude.

The ice around us was four or five feet in thickness ; but the pieces were in general small, seldom exceeding forty feet in extent. From the sand and gravel, and also pieces of rock on the ice, it is probable that the masses came from the islands scattered over the northern parts of Baffin's Bay. This is confirmed by the southerly setting of the current and ice in which the ships were carried along. At last, on the morning of *Wednesday* the 30th, the ice slackened enough to permit us to force our way through it to the eastward into clear sea ; and on the following morning we again made way to the northward. Painful as was the long delay thus occasioned while beset in the ice, the time was not unprofitably spent. Several new birds, new I mean to some of us, passed under review, one called the burgo-master by the Dutch seamen, from his domineering over his fellow birds as that ruler or mayor governs his fellowmen in Holland. Near one of the icebergs we saw several puffins, or Greenland parrots as the seamen call them. The ivory gull also came in sight for the first time; but it might be better named the snow gull, for the snow itself scarcely excels it in brilliancy of colours. A large black whale for the first time raised his head to take breath near the ships, on Sunday the 27th, and gave no small amusement to such of our company as had been in the Greenland fishery, by his going down tail foremost between two pieces of ice; for the animal found it could not turn over to go down in the usual way, the head first. While the wind was strong it kept the ice together so that the ships lay snug; but when it abated a long heavy swell of the sea came in from the westward, which drove the masses of ice against the ship's side and stern with a force sufficient to endanger, perhaps destroy, any vessel not carefully strengthened with wood and iron as ours were. Early in the morning of the 28th a large white bear appeared very near us, and was wounded by some shot; but he soon afterwards fell down between two blocks of ice and was lost; for on being severely wounded the bear instantly sinks. His appearance in such a spot shows to what a distance those animals venture out to sea; for we must at this time have been many leagues off from any land. The smelling of this animal is exceedingly acute, and he was probably attracted towards the ship by the smell of some red herrings frying for the men on board. At least it is by such an operation that the bears are drawn near the ships in the whale fishery. The swell abated, but the ships continued fast in the ice on the 29th, when we discovered land to the westward, probably towards the entrance of Cumberland Strait on the American side. The depth of water in this place was above 130 fathoms, where the temperature was 30° the same with that at the surface; while the air was at 84°. The land in sight was probably about fourteen leagues off. On the 30th the ice loosened a little, and the ships, by several hours' severe towing and warping, at last forced their way back again into clear water, on the east of the ice. Thus failed our first attempt to make good our way towards the western shore of Davis's Strait; an object particularly recommended to us, as I have understood, before we left England. It is, besides, by running along the west coast that we can hope to discover a passage, to lead us across the North American seas, to our destined point, Behring's strait, between America and Asia.

When we returned into open sea, our Greenland masters were uncertain which course to hold, to obtain a more practicable course through the ice; at last it was determined to stand to the northward, between the ice and Greenland.

Monday, 5th July.—The most noticeable occurrence in these days past, has been our entrance within the arctic circle, at four in the afternoon of Saturday the 3d, in west long. 57° 27′. This famous circle, you know, bounds the space within which the sun never sets or never rises, for a longer or shorter time, according to the season of the year, and according as you advance more or less towards the pole.

The arctic circle, and its opposite the antarctic, are supposed to be described round the poles, with a radius equal to the chord of 23½ degrees, equal to the distance of the tropics of Cancer and Capricorn, N. or S. from the equator. Owing to the thickness of the weather we could not follow the sun's motion round the horizon, yet for some days before we actually crossed the Arctic circle, such was the strength of the twilight, even at midnight, that we were enabled to see to a considerable distance round the ship, and to discover in which way we should steer to get the soonest clear of ice. In the course of the 3d we saw or passed upwards of 40 icebergs, some of them of great size. In the night the wind fell, and turned to the SW., leaving us at the mercy of the heavy swell from the southward, which drove the loose ice against the lofty bergs with prodigious force and noise. The situation of the ships, particularly of the Hecla, which was the farthest advanced, was now very critical: but by means of some hours' hard pulling in the boats, she was brought back into clear water, and the Griper was prevented from entering much among the ice. While close to these bergs, no bottom was found at the depth of 110 fathoms.

At noon of the 4th we had made lat. 66° 41′, and lon. 56° 48′, being about the middle of the narrowest part of Davis's Strait. In the account of his third voyage he says the strait was there in breadth 40 leagues, and that in lat. 67° he could see America on the one hand, and Greenland, (which he very properly termed Desolation,) on the other. The truth of this remark has been long doubted ; but the expedition of 1818, under Captain Ross, established its accuracy; this part of the Strait being ascertained not to exceed fifty leagues in breadth, from E. to W

While the Hecla was contending with the dense bodies of floating ice, the necessity of employing a ship of large size and power, to force her way through, was very evident. The Griper herself would often have been arrested had not the Hecla cleared the way before her.

On the 5th we saw a walrus, or sea-horse as it is called, although in no way resembling the land horse, on the ice ; and on the following day a number were observed crowded together, at some distance from the ships. A party in a boat approached very near to them unobserved ; whether owing to the stupidity of the animals, or to their being asleep. At last the largest, which lay in front, raising his head, roused his comrades, and all began to tumble off the ice into the sea. The party in the boat severely wounded the largest, which sunk, but quickly rose again, when he was dispatched with a harpoon, a kind of javelin used in killing whales: to secure him, however, a second blow was necessary. The comrades of the wounded animal, as we were told by the Greenland men on board, usually make an effort to rescue him, by attacking the common enemy; but on this occasion nothing of that sort was attempted. Not having been one of the party myself, I am sorry that I cannot speak so precisely respecting the manners of the walrus as you and as I could wish: I can, however, give some notion of the size and general appearance of the animal we killed. The length of the animal from the snout to the end of the hind flippers, or feet, was 10 feet 3 inches; the girth round the body, behind the fore-flippers, 6 feet 10 inches; circuit of the neck 4 feet 5 inches; full extent of fore-flippers 5 feet 10 inches; that of hind-flippers 4 feet 10 inches. Both fore and hind flippers had each five toes, joined like those of a duck. Length of the two tusks which descend from the upper jaw 5 inches. No external ears. The hair on the body thin and coarse; the colour a dark bay on the back, but lighter on the sides: the under part of the body mottled, not unlike the common seal. Such is the account given by the gentlemen who examined the walrus with particular care. The weight of the whole carcase was 1400 pounds. As it is chiefly by means of their tusks that the walruses draw themselves up on the ice, it is no wonder that they are sometimes found without one or both of the tusks. The walrus is reported to wage mortal combat with the white, or polar bear. The walrus seems to be the same animal with the sea lion, so frequent at the southern extremity of South America. As an article of food, nothing but the most absolute want of sustenance can ever induce any person of civilized life to eat it. Under the skin is a coat of fat, similar to the blubber of the whale, from two to three inches in thickness; and the flesh below is as black as that of the whale, and so disgusting, that even the dogs on board would not touch it. The fat, or blubber, was casked up, to be boiled, and furnish oil for lamps in the dark winter.

In standing to the northward on the 7th, we came to a stream of ice which required several hours rowing of the boats to draw the ships through it. Here, as on former occasions, it was remarked that when we came under the lee of ice, whatever was its height above the water, if only a single foot, the strength of the wind always abated. The cause of this it is not easy to explain.

On *Tuesday* the 6th, we were able for the first time to take the altitude of the sun above the horizon at midnight, or more properly between the horizon and the pole-star; for as the sun never sets, there can be strictly speaking no night. The effect is curious to the inhabitant of the southern latitudes; but as it came on gradually, the sun wheeling round, and his obscuration daily diminishing, the phenomenon struck me less than I had imagined would be the case. Since the sun has ceased to set, the term night has become of no signification.

On the 10th came on a very dense fog, which occasioned serious apprehensions, as many icebergs were near us. It is however fortunate that even in the thickest fog the reflection of the light from those prodigious masses of ice is so strong, that, when the water is smooth, you may with proper attention be able to steer clear of them. One great inconvenience arising from the fog, however, was its freezing on the rigging, which rendered the management of the sails and ropes not only difficult but painful to the men.

On the forenoon of the 11th, a large bear was observed on a piece of floating ice near our track, which was killed and brought on board by a boat's crew. To obtain possession of these animals the Greenland seamen are very expert in throwing a rope round his neck; for, as was mentioned before, as soon as wounded the bear plunges into the sea. This he also does for the purpose of attacking his foes in the boat, by laying his paw on her side. The greenland boats are so built and managed that he is seldom able to overset them: but the boats of our ships are of a very different construction, and might be easily upset by his force and weight.

This bear measured in length from snout to tail eight feet two inches; the circumference round the middle was 6 feet; height from heel of fore paw to top of shoulders 3 feet 7 inches; the fore leg measured 2 feet 5 inches round below the knee. The front teeth of both jaws were 6 inches long, the grinders 5 inches. The whole weight, notwithstanding his great size, was only 895 pounds; for the animal was found to be very lean and far gone in disease.

The best weapon our people employed against a bear, when attempting this operation, was the pike used in boarding an enemy's ship; for unless you be very near, a musket ball will not always have its intended effect. As we coasted the ice northwards many seals were seen, but very seldom two together, a circumstance the opposite of the custom of the walrus, although they seem to be animals much of the same kind.

On *Monday* the 12th, the weather was foggy, but the sun being visible, Captain Parry and Captain Sabine ascended an iceberg to observe his meridian altitude. By it the latitude appeared to be 69° 43′, and the longitude 57° 46′. On the 15th, the fog being still dense, our latitude was found by observation to be 70° 27′ 43″, and our longitude 59° 11′ 58″. The variation of the needle on the ice, at such a distance from the ship as to be out of the sphere of her attraction, was now 79° 48′ westerly.

An experiment was made in the Hecla to discover the relative weight of the ice of a berg and the sea water. A cubical piece of ice 5¾ inches a side was immersed in a vessel of water; when the ice floated, leaving two-thirds of an inch of the cube above the surface. Pure distilled fresh water being the standard or 1, the sea-water weighed 1 0256: the temperature of the water in the vessel was 33°.

Friday 16th.—Passed the Brunswick of Hull, and learned that a large fleet of whale ships were stopt about latitude 74° by the ice in Baffin's Bay. From the observations of the gentlemen on board, who were in the expedition of last year, it seems probable that ships entering Davis's Straits in the first days of July may penetrate as far as latitude 75°, without any retardment from the ice; and, perhaps, a good deal higher. For some days past flocks of eider ducks, from whom we steal their delicate down, provided by nature for the comfort of their young families, have past us on the wing for the eastward. On the 17th, judging from some appearances that clear sea was at no great distance to the westward, another attempt was made to break through the ice in that direction. But the wind, which was favourable, as usual died away, and we were again obliged to return to our track on the east of the ice. In forcing our way by the boats, across a narrow but dense stream of ice, in our course northwards, one of the Hecla's boats overset; but the people got upon the ice after only a hearty dipping.

This day the ships' companies were employed in laying in a supply of water from the surface of the ice; for from the climate of the country to which we are bound, it cannot be expected that any other than melted snow or ice can ever be procured.

The weather being quite calm on the 20th, with a thick fog, a current setting to the SSW carried the ships right towards a very considerable iceberg, at the same time that a large quantity of floating ice was moving the same way. By means of the boats we were carried clear of the berg just before the floating ice completely surrounded it. To give you some idea of these bergs, conceive to yourself that this mass of primeval ice rose 140 feet above the surface of the sea, at the same time that it was fast aground in the depth of 120 fathoms, or 720 feet. The whole height of this berg must therefore have been 860 feet. This was not all; for the side next to the ship actually overhung the water, projecting beyond the perpendicular. The berg was besides rent in a multitude of places, presenting unquestionable indications of its being ready to split and overwhelm any vessel that should unfortunately be near it.

On the 21st, *Wednesday*, the fog dispersing exhibited to us a tolerably distinct view of the Greenland coast to the eastward. The part we saw was supposed to be that called Hope Sanderson, with some of the Women's Islands, mentioned by Davis. This land, distant probably about 40 miles, was the first we had seen for an extent of 10° of latitude since we entered the Strait. In this position, from 80 to 90 icebergs could be counted from the ships at one time, some of them of great size, and probably aground in very deep water. From these bergs streams of pure water generally proceed, and even on the plains and patches of ice pools of it were found. The masses are consequently in a state of gradual diminution. The sun being constantly above the horizon, must no doubt warm the air and promote the solution of the ice. Persons on board of our ship, however, who have repeatedly visited the arctic regions, agree in the opinion of the illustrious Cook and Burney, that the sea is the great dissolver of the ice. One may, indeed, be convinced, without a voyage to the polar regions, that water in its fluid state must be always at a higher temperature than when congealed. The bergs, therefore, which sink deep in the sea, or in general about seven times as much as they rise above the surface, must in the immersed part be in a state of gradual decay. The base being thus diminished, the superstructure in the course of ages is undermined, crumbles down and mingles with the waters of the ocean. Dangerous to shipping as are the icebergs, still they are not without their advantages. When a ship is beset or inclosed in the floating ice, it is of great service to secure her to the largest berg or body of ice which can be obtained: she thus is less removed from her position, for the deeper the berg sinks in the water the less it is exposed to be driven from its place, even if afloat. Another advantage is this, that in proportion to the extent of the berg, the larger is the space of clear sea under its lee, or opposite to that side on which the drift bears.

Struggling in this manner with the ice, availing ourselves of every favourable turn of the wind or of the currents, we at last, at noon of Tuesday the 27th, with a fresh breeze from the south-eastward, managed to gain northward and westward into latitude 73°.06′., and longitude 60° 21′¼. The ice now assumed a different appearance from that to the eastward and southward. It was chiefly what is called bay or young ice, probably newly formed in the sheltered spots among the great bodies.

Through this thin ice the ships forced their way, at the rate of from four to five miles in the hour. In the midst of their course, however, we had at times the mortification to be stopt by what is called a field of ice ; that is a mass of great thickness, so extended that its bounds can not be discovered from the mast-head. On this occasion, one field we met with was not less than ten feet in thickness. In mentioning the mast-head, I ought rather to have said the crow's nest, which is the name given by the whalers to a cask or similar frame, fixed at the mast-head, in which the look-out man sits, tolerably sheltered from the weather, to discover land or whales, and to direct the ship in making her way through the ice. No such field I understand, was seen in the former voyage in these seas. From this ice the ships received many blows in the course of the day, which however did them no apparent danger, nor do even our delicate time-keepers or chronometers appear to have been injured by the shocks. It was remarked on board that, after we lost sight of Greenland, few or no icebergs came in our way ; this is ascribed to the great depth of the water, which prevents them from grounding ; the depth being in various places nearly 300 fathoms.

Wednesday 28th. The wind coming away hard from SE. with much rain, we at last quite cleared the great body of ice which, stretching from N. to S. in the middle of Baffin's bay, cuts off in a manner all communication between the east and west coasts. Our course across this ice, in the direction about WNW. ¼ W. extended full 80 miles ; nor had any ship ever passsed over in the same latitude, at the same time of the year. In the operation, however, we were greatly indebted to the strong SE. winds, and to the excellent construction of the Hecla, which opened the way for the less powerful Griper. I ought to mention that, on account of the very severe and almost incessant labour of the men, an extra allowance of spirits was repeatedly served out to them, together with a quantity of preserved meat, which we carried out from England.

Thursday 29th. Having got now into clear water, the ships pitched in a manner to show that the sea before us was open to a considerable extent; for when the ice prevails the waves have not room to produce that motion. We were at noon in lat. 73° 51' and long. 67° 48', sufficiently to the northward to open the entrance of Lancaster's Sound, the grand object of our present research and hopes. At half past five in the afternoon of *Friday* the 30th, we at last got the joyful sight of the high land, at the S. point of the entrance of the sound. The exultation produced on all on board, by this sight, it is impossible for me to paint. We were now arrived at the solution of the grand question of the existence of a passage through, or at least far into that inlet of the sea ; and the anxiety of those even who had the least hesi tation respecting its existence was raised to the highest pitch. The object was in a manner new to me; but it would have been strange indeed if I had not been infected with the enthusiasm of all around me. The Hecla, which was a-head, signified the discovery of land to the Griper, and both ships set all sail they could, as if they had contended which should first gain the desired object. Preparations were now made on board both ships for coming to anchor, when a proper opportunity or necessity should offer: but as it is observed that the wind usually blows right up or down the great inlets of these seas, it came away so much from the westward, out of the sound, that we made but little way in that direction.

This morning, however, (*Saturday* 31st July) we stood in for the land, and sounded 80 fathoms on a rocky bottom, 2 miles E. from a lofty broad head-land, a little to the northward of Possession bay, so named from possession being taken of it in the former expedition under Captain Ross. The flag-staff then erected on a mount on the shore of the bay was gladly saluted by all on board, who hastened on deck to recognise it as an old friend. As we approached Lancaster Sound the number of whales around were prodigious: upwards of 80 were counted in the course of yesterday, and in general of a large size. So at least they were considered by our Greenland masters on board. It is a general notion in the Greenland fishery that the whales are not to be expected where there is no ice: there is no rule however without exceptions; and in this case where the whales were in the greatest numbers no ice was within sight. The Griper had been taken in tow for some time by the Hecla, when they had cleared the ice in the middle of the bay: but the wind coming away strong from the westward she was cast off, and was therefore considerably behind the Hecla in getting in with the land. To turn this delay to some advantage, Captain Parry, with Captain Sabine and Mr. Fisher the surgeon, landed from the Hecla in Possession bay, near the mouth of the stream, where observations were made in the former. The Latitude of this spot is 73° 31′ 16″ N. and its Longitude by the chronometers 77° 22′ 21″ W. The variation of magnetic needle was found to be 108° 47′, or 9⅔ points of the compass to the westward of the true north. The westerly deviation of the magnetic meridian, at the entrance of Sir James Lancaster's sound, is therefore nearly five times as much as it is on the E. coast of Britain: the vertical dip of the needle 86° 4′. It was remarked by some of the gentlemen who were here in the last expedition, that the mountains around Possession bay seemed to have considerably more snow on them now than on that occasion. This may perhaps be owing to our coming on the coast a month earlier than on that occasion. For the greatest heat and the greatest cold are always found sometime after the longest and the shortest day; less snow may therefore be found on the mountains here in the end of July than in the end of August. From the same cause the stream which falls into the sea in the bottom of Possession bay, which, like other arctic streams, is produced by the melting of the snow in the environs, was found to be very low. The mean temperature of the air in the shade at noon was 37° 08'; that of the sea at the surface 32° 6': the barometer stood at 29.505 inches; the wind NW. by W. fresh breeze and fine weather.

Pieces of birch bark having been found in the bed of the stream in 1818, it was supposed to denote the existence of trees of that sort, and perhaps of others in the vicinity. No trees of any kind were however discovered in a walk of about four miles up the stream: the bark, therefore, in question, was undoubtedly conveyed thither by some visitors of the Esquimaux nations, of whom some other memorials were found. The time of high water on full and change of the moon seemed to be at a quarter past 11. A. M. and the rise of the tide on those days may be from six to eight feet. The flood-tide comes from the N. and W. along the coast. In proceeding up the stream, human footsteps were traced as perfect as if they had been impressed but a few days before. On better consideration, however, it seemed beyond a doubt that they had remained from the preceding voyage, when persons belonging to that expedition had traversed the same ground in search of objects of natural history. The only animals seen to-day, on shore, were a fox, a raven, some ring-plovers and snow-buntings: a solitary bee was also observed on the wing. Wherever moisture prevailed, tufts of grass and some other plants were found in plenty: but the only growth of the tree kind was the creeping, ground, or dwarf willow, the thickest of which did not exceed a finger. The rocks consisted of basalt and granite; but in the valley were many loose fragments of limestone. The water near the shore of the bay deepens rapidly; for the depth was fourteen fathoms, on a sandy bottom, within the length of a cable or 120 fathoms of the beach.

The flag staff erected on Possession mount was still entire; but a pile of stones was collected on the side of the stream, at a sufficient distance back from the shore, under which was placed a bottle with a paper containing the date and the names of the ships and the commanders.

The boats are now returned from the shore, and all hands are preparing for our eventful attempt to penetrate Lancaster's Sound. I must therefore bid you all adieu for some little time to come.

Ever Your's, &c. &c.

LETTER VI.

Lancaster's Sound, Wednesday
1st September, 1819.

WELL do I know, my dear Thomas, that no incident, no operation on board ship, since I left London, however uninteresting to a stranger, will be passed over by you and my other friends at home, as of little importance or unworthy of notice. The transactions and occurrences noticed in my letters hitherto, have in them, nevertheless, nothing new, nothing extraordinary, nothing but what may, and doubtless often does happen, to all who navigate the seas which we have traversed. Our adventures among the hills and shoals of ice, which occupy the middle portion of Davis's Strait and Baffin's Bay, are, however, certainly out of the ordinary course of sea affairs; for it was necessary that we should quit the usual track of shipping bound for those quarters; because the object for which the expedition was fitted out, is of a nature very different from those contemplated in the commercial enterprises of our countrymen, or of the mariners of other nations, who resort to the northern seas.

I am now to commence my remarks on a region hitherto unknown, or at any rate certainly undescribed by any navigator. This is the inlet of the sea opening into Baffin's Bay, on the west side, called Sir James Lancaster's Sound; the nature of which has, for many years, and in particular since the return of the expedition of 1818, occasioned no small diversity of opinion, among men of geographical and nautical science. The term *sound*, employed by Baffin, has sometimes been supposed to signify an inlet of the sea, but not a passage communicating with the open sea at the opposite extremity. If, however, we look to the application of the term in known cases, we find that it is, in fact, just what now-a-days we call a *strait*. Thus we have the Sound of Elsineur, leading from the Atlantic into the Baltic, between Denmark and Sweden. Nearer home we have the Sound of Mull, which separates that island from the continent of Scotland. In embarking on an expedition, for the purpose of determining the true nature of Lancaster's Sound, therefore, the anxiety which occupies every one engaged is beyond description: to conceive it, indeed, it requires to be felt. You will, of course, readily forgive me, if at once I return to my own dull matter-of-fact mode of relating things and notions as they present themselves to my notice. One thing I must, however, mention, which occasions very serious uneasiness to us all. This is, that the Griper, which at first kept a pretty equal pace with the Hecla, when sailing on a wind,

seems now to have fallen off very sensibly in that good property.
The consequence will be, that the Hecla must either slacken her
course, in order to have the Griper in company, and thereby lose
invaluable time in this most inhospitable quarter of the globe, or
be reduced to the cruel necessity of abandoning her consort, and
pursuing the expedition alone. But *spero meliora*—you see, my
good fellow, I have not yet quite forgotten my Latin.

On *Sunday* the 1*st August*, we endeavoured, by standing away
to the northward from Possession Bay and its vicinity, to make
at least an entrance into the broad opening of Lancaster's Sound.
The wind was, however, right out of the sound, accompanied by
a heavy swell in the same direction; so that at noon of the 2d
we had gained but very little westing, when we came into lat. 74°
30', and long. 78° 1', the north point of the sound bearing about
W by N. distant forty miles. The weather being clear in the
evening, when, by turning up to the westward, we had gained about
midway between the entrance points of the sound, we had a
tolerably distinct view of the lands on both sides. That on the
south appeared mountainous and rugged, while the north coast
was less elevated and uneven. This side was, of course, less involved in snow than the opposite. Numbers of black whales
were seen around us, with the peculiarity of many young ones;
contrary to what is remarked by the whale-fishers, who, it is said,
very seldom meet with young fish any where excepting on the
coasts of East Greenland and Spitzbergen. If this be the case,
it would seem to denote, that the general nursery of the young
whales is situated much nearer to the pole than our position;
and that the communication between that nursery and East
Greenland is much more convenient for the fish than that with
Baffin's Bay. Hence, perhaps, we may suppose the vast region
of Greenland to be insulated alike from America as from Asia.
Every thing seems to announce a range of open sea before us to
the westward. The icebergs may be said to have disappeared,
and the ice which we see floating is too close to the north coast to
offer any obstacle to our progress. The water has changed its
colour since we entered the sound, from its usual light green to
a dirty brownish tinge. At 9, A. M. of *Monday* the 2d, in the
middle of the entrance, the sounding-line gave 1050 fathoms,
on a bottom of mud and small stones. The real depth, however,
did not, perhaps, go beyond 850 or 900 fathoms (an English
mile); for, in the calmest weather, the weight of the line itself
will continue to draw it out, even after the lead has reached the
bottom; hence, reported great depths of the sea must be received
with caution.

Tuesday 3*d*.—While the Hecla was contending against breezes
from the westward and calms, the Griper, which had fallen

behind eight or nine miles, had a brisk wind from the westward. This carried her forward to join her consort which, on receiving the same breeze, crowded all sail to push on westward. Expectation was now raised to the highest pitch, to look out to discover whether the passage up the sound was obstructed by either land or ice : but nothing of the kind appeared.

In the forenoon of the 3d we had a view of the north coast of the sound, from Hope's monument (a remarkable conical hill, now found to be on the land, and not an island, as it had appeared on the former voyage,) westward to Cape Warrender, a bold headland advancing into the sound. Being at noon in lat. 74° 26', and long. 80° $4\frac{1}{2}'$, the magnetic variation was found to be only 106° 58' westerly. This last quantity is very remarkable; for it would indicate a diminution of the variation which had regularly increased during the whole voyage from England. We were still going to the westward, and, consequently, drawing nearer to the supposed position of the magnetic pole of the earth. The observation was, besides, made on one of the very few icebergs now within sight, where no local attraction from the minerals, either in the ships or in the ground, could, in any way, affect the needle of the compass. In Possession Bay the variation was 108° 47', and we had now increased our long. 2° 42'; yet the deviation of the needle from the meridian lessened 1° 49'; but the variation itself is known to vary in the course of a single day.

From Cape Warrender the north coast trended north-westerly, leading into a deep bay or inlet, which was named after Mr. Croker, Secretary of the Admiralty. The land appeared composed of high mountains, in some parts of that level kind, called by seamen table-land. Being nearly in the meridian of Cape Castlereagh, on the south coast, but above forty miles off, we could observe a deep bay, or inlet, on its west side, which was named Navy Board Inlet. Both this and Croker Bay may, perhaps, be only openings between insulated portions of the land. The cape on the west side of the latter bay was named after Sir Everard Home.

The wind being fresh from the east, and the sea unencumbered, except by a few icebergs, seemingly much decayed, the Hecla soon got nearly out of sight of the Griper; and the weather being extremely clear, she before dark had got to the vicinity of the position where land was supposed to be seen across the sound in the expedition of last year, namely, about the meridian of west long. 83°. In the course of this day's run breakers were seen to the northward, near to lat. 85°, intimating the presence of rocks in that spot. The broken water might, however, have been produced by a multitude of loose masses of ice; for the Griper found seventy-five fathoms water on sand and mud near the spot. This depth is, nevertheless, much less than what had been found in any other part of the run up the sound.

Wednesday 4*th*.—In the morning the Griper got up to the Hecla in the meridian of lat. 85°, the place previously fixed for the meeting of the ships in the middle of the sound, in case of separation. Still not the smallest indication of land, in our course to the westward, could be perceived. The sea was quite free from any connected ice, to announce its connexion with the shore, and all apprehensions of disappointment in our project of making our way good along the seas of North America were nearly dispelled, when, about six in the morning, we were stunned by the alarm that land was seen a head. Our mortification was not, however, of long duration; for, as we advanced, and the weather brightened, the land was found to be an island of no great size on our left, towards the south shore of the sound. On each side of it the horizon was perfectly clear. Standing still on to the westward, our progress was at once cut short by a connected body of ice, which extended across the whole breadth of the strait, to a cape forming the west point of Maxwell Bay on the north coast. The wind was carrying the ships fast down upon this ice, where they must have been inclosed, had we not hauled off to the northward, to a proper distance. Another island was then discovered to the south of the first; and both were distinguished by the names of Prince Leopold's Islands; the north one being in lat. 74°, and long. 90°. In looking southward, to the east of these islands, we perceived what the northern seamen call a water-sky: that is, a dark appearance of the sky, denoting water under it in that quarter. For over ice or snow the sky assumes a peculiar brightness, called ice or snow blink, which may be seen at a considerable distance; the land-blink is, generally, more of a yellow hue than that over ice.

For some time before we reached Prince Leopold's Islands the south coast of the sound was hidden by a thick haze; but of the north coast we had a sufficient view all along. There the land has a very peculiar appearance, being perpendicular and very high over the sea, probably not less than five hundred feet. The strata of these precipices are laid open to view, and regularly horizontal, but of very unequal thickness. The outer face is separated by vertical fissures, into ranges of natural buttresses, which give the coast the air of an immense stretch of decayed walls and towers. It is intersected by many openings or inlets, giving to various parts more the appearance of a succession of islands, all lofty, precipitous, and inaccessible, than of a continued tract of sea-coast. That the land on the north, and, indeed, on both sides of the sound, may turn out to be a group of islands, is not at all improbable. In the evening of the 4th, the white whales, a pecular species, were seen for the first time: various kinds of sea-fowl were also observed in numbers, near the edges of the ice. From the northernmost of the Leopold isles, the distance over to the north coast may be about thirty miles north and south. Although the interior of the country on the north coast was lofty, and even mountainous, yet not so much snow was seen on it as might have been expected. This has been accounted for by persons not such strangers to arctic lands as I am, by the surface being in general plain, on which the drifting winds have full scope for their violence, to carry off the snow and lodge it in the deep ravines and gullies, which, no doubt, intersect the land, but which are not to be seen from sea.

Thursday 5th.—The weather was too foggy to allow us to make any attempt to turn, or to force a passage through some opening of the ice; and the east wind falling off, we had light shifting airs with thick drifting snow. As, in these circumstances, we could only endeavour to maintain the position we had gained, for, while the Hecla could discover no current in any direction, the Griper found one setting eastward, at the rate of nine or ten miles in the day, attempts were made, but in vain, to strike some of the white whales. For they would dive before the boats could get within forty yards of them. They seemed to be, in general, towards twenty feet long; and sometimes, while under water, a singular *whistling* noise proceeded from them, which our seamen, with their characteristic skill in giving names to objects, called the *whale-song*. White whales are mentioned by the adventurous Mackenzie, as being seen at the mouth of the river which he traced down to the sea, on the north coast of North America, and which now in its name records his exploit; may not this fact show the straits, in which we are now entangled, to communicate directly with Mackenzie's sea? This day, also, for the first time in the voyage, and for the first time in my life, we saw that curious fish, called in the northern seas the narwhal, and by our people the sea-unicorn. Should we have the good luck to gain possession of one of these formidable gentry of the north, you shall have some account of him.

Saturday 7th.—No opening in the ice appearing on the north of Prince Leopold's isles, our attention was directed to the southward, where the water-sky announced the absence of land. We were, however, still detained off those islands by calms, and the ice, which extended several miles from them, prevented all attempts to land upon them. This was, however, of the less importance, for they must have been wholly inaccessible, being surrounded, wherever we saw, by lofty perpendicular precipices, exhibiting regular horizontal strata, forming shelves, as it were, round the cliffs, but none of the buttresses which distinguish the

N. coast of the Sound. On board the Griper the calm weather was employed in shifting her topmasts which had been sprung by carrying a press of sail, to keep up with the Hecla.

One of the boats of the Hecla was upset by the fall of some ice which the people were collecting near the islands, to be disolved on board for use : but no injury was done. Ice from a berg is always chosen for the purpose ; but that on large bodies of floating ice, although it be in fact the ice of sea-water, answers very well when the salt water is allowed to drain off. Agreeably to the general remark that a bold, that is a lofty steep projecting coast is usually accompanied by deep water near the land, the soundings off the Leopoldine isles passed speedily from 135 to 175 fathoms on a bottom of soft mud. In the afternoon yesterday, the fog wearing away to the southward, we had a sight of the coast in the SE. quarter. A breeze then coming away from the NNW. both ships stood to the southward into what soon appeared to be a spacious inlet of the sea, at least ten leagues wide at the entrance, and opening up in a direction towards SSW. As far as could be discovered the coasts had no tendency to meet, nor was there the faintest indications of land in the bottom. The W. coast was in beset with ice that, however anxious we were to penetrate in that direction, no operation of that kind seemed at all practicable; we therefore ran southward between the ice and the E. coast, in a broad open channel for about two degrees of Latitude, or 120 miles.

Among the mysteries of nature by which men are environed, none is more interesting, because none is more essential to the navigator, than the powers and the properties of the magnet. That the needle when magnetized, and at liberty to move freely, regards a pole different from the poles of the earth, has long been known. But this is not all. This deviation, or variation, as it is termed, is itself subject to gradual variation; and it is only from continued observation of the effects produced by this double change of position of the needle of the mariner's compass that its position and indications can from time to time be known. When the polarity of the magnetized needle was first observed in London it pointed to the E. of the true north ; that is, the variation was easterly. In the course of years, drawing more and more westward, the magnetic meridian at last coincided with the terrestrial, and no variation existed. Continuing to move westward, the magnet pointed above two points W. from the true north. This was the case a few years ago, when the needle became stationary, and now it seems to be returning eastward to coincide once more with the true north. On the 18th of May the variation on the N. coast of Scotland was found to be 26° 38′ westerly ; on the 23rd June, at the beginning of the ice in Davis's Strait 61° 26′; on the 31st

July, in Possession bay, at the S. point of Lancaster's Sound 108° 47'. Ever since we entered the Sound the irregularities proceeding from the local attractions in the ships, the sluggishness of the needles, the change in their dip, have become so important and embarrassing, increasing as we advanced westward in the strait, as to render the compasses of no real use; circumstances all seeming to announce our approach to the present magnetic pole. It became therefore of the utmost importance, to ascertain by observations either on a solid field of ice or on the land, the true variation and dip of the needle. Lieutenants Beechey of the Hecla, and Hoppner of the Griper, with Captain Sabine, who acted in the capacity of astronomer, and Mr. Fisher, assistant surgeon of the Hecla, were therefore landed on the E. coast, some miles within the entrance of the inlet. The coast was low on the water, and rose to no great elevation, nor could be termed mountainous in the interior. Little snow was seen, but the soil seemed to be of the most sterile description. Some tufts of grass by the brooks, a poppy or two of very poor growth, and common moss or lichens, were the only vegetable productions met with. The only animals seen were a brace of ptarmigans and some snow buntings. On the beach were found some seal bones, and some white hair resembling that of the arctic fox. The rocks in places were chiefly limestone; but fragments of granite, hornblend, and quartz, were scattered on the shore. The bed of a stream consisted of clay slate, although the banks were calcareous. Along the beach lay a range of large pieces of ice, in some places ten feet thick. Judging from the fall of the tide during the stay on the land, the water seemed to rise from twelve to fourteen feet. The ebb set to the southward, from which quarter of course the flood-tide must proceed. The water in the stream indicated a temperature of $42\frac{1}{2}°$, the air in the shade $51\frac{1}{2}°$, and the earth near the surface $34\frac{1}{4}°$. No remains of huts or any other signs of human beings were observed, a want which our officers supplied; for on a hill, near the landing place, they erected a pole with a board on which they painted the date and the names of the ships. Near this pole a bottle was buried, containing a similar notice in writing at greater length. The weather being remarkably clear, our ships continued under sail through the night; for the sun at midnight just dipped below the horizon, and rose again a few minutes afterwards. The water of the inlet now changed to pale green and very deep; we found 35 fathoms within three miles of the shore. Standing on still southward, the dark colour of the sky announced clear water in that direction, and the inlet evidently widened; but early in the morning of the 8th, the ice, hitherto confined to the west coast, stretched over to the east shore to a point of land which seemed to terminate that shore. This point was named after

Captain Kater, who has so greatly improved the compass and the pendulum: its position is in latitude 71° 53½' and longitude 90° 04'. From all the circumstances observed in this inlet, it seemed to be the opinion on board, that it certainly communicates with the open sea to the southward, and that by watching the state of the ice in that direction a vessel may make good her way westward along before the rivers seen by Hearne and Mackenzie: perhaps, find a passage south-eastwardly into Hudson's Bay.

No passage appearing practicable through this inlet to the southward, the ships returned to Lancaster's Sound, in which it was hoped some opening might present itself through the ice between Prince Leopold's Islands and the north shore. While we were near Cape Kater, in the inlet, the magnet became of less use than ever before, for even in that gentleman's improved steering compasses the north point of the needle pointed constantly to the ship's head in whatever position she was placed. On our return northward, we found the ice to have closed much over towards the east coast of the inlet; and thick weather coming on with snow, the ships were made fast to it. Here we laid in a complete stock of excellent water from the pools on the floating ice, waiting until the weather should clear up and the wind become favourable, which we had before observed to blow either right up or down the inlet.

Thursday being the 12th of August, the birth-day of His Royal Highness the Prince Regent, it naturally suggested to affix his name to the inlet. On the following morning we were opposite to an opening in the east coast, running in a little to the southward of east. It was a mile over at the mouth, and three miles deep. About the middle of the north side a small island formed a very safe anchorage; for it was joined to the land by a ledge of rocks which kept out both sea and ice. The water in the whole bay was very deep; in the anchorage it was from five to eight fathoms very near the land, which is every where steep, excepting in the bottom of the bay, where a stream falls in, which comes down through a most barren tract covered with loose fragments of limestone. The bay, which was named Port Bowen, lies in latitude 73° 12' 11″, and longitude 89° 2' 8″. The variation at three miles out from the land was 114° 17' westerly.

A light breeze in the evening of the 13th carried the ships north to Prince Leopold's Islands, which proved to be more inclosed with ice than when we stood to the southward. While we were in the inlet many white whales and some black ones were seen. Narwhals, or sea-unicorns, also were swimming about in vast numbers. On this account the Greenland masters on board thought a fishing establishment in that inlet could not fail to be very profitable, for the oil of the fish and the ivory of the narwhal's horn—*à propos* of the narwhal ;—I am now able to fulfil my promise, respecting this curious animal, one of which was killed by a party from the Hecla and taken on board on Wednesday the 11th. The narwhal differs in general shape from the whale in this, that, like most other fish, the thickest part of the body is towards the middle of the length, whereas, in the whale it is very near the head. What is called the horn is properly a piece of bone or ivory, which projects from the snout : in this case it was united to the left side, but on the other side no vestige of a horn appeared, as is sometimes observed. The horn, which is generally in length about one-third of that of the body, tapers to a point, being surrounded by a spiral indent which looks as if it were twisted. In our fish the length of the horn was four feet two inches, but some inches of it seemed to have been broken off : the circumference at the root $5\frac{1}{4}$ inches, at the top $2\frac{2}{3}$ inches. Length of fish from horn to tail $13\frac{1}{4}$ feet : circumference of thickest part of body about 9 feet. The female, as I hear, has no horns. The narwhal has no teeth, so that, like the whale, the food must be of a very soft nature. The tongue of both fish is of the same kind, being only a mass of soft fat attached to the under part of the mouth, consequently, quite unfit to promote mastication. The tail and fins, like those of the whale, differ from those other fish in consisting of gristly fat covered with skin, as is the body. The skin, which is half an inch in thickness, covers a layer of blubber from three to four inches in substance, and in this fish was supposed to be in sufficient quantity to produce above sixty gallons of oil. The flesh was black and of a fragile nature. In the internal parts the narwhal, like the whale, perfectly resembles land animals of the mammalia class. Large as the animal was, the stomach contained nothing but a greenish oily liquid.

The ice to the westward affording no means of prosecuting our course that way, a boat from each ship went ashore on the 15th, at the north-east point of the Prince Regent's inlet. The ground was equally barren with that further south, consisting generally of limestone containing fossil shells. On the top of a hill, about 700 feet above the sea, a bottle was placed under a pile of stones containing the date of our arrival at the spot. From this hill no water was seen beyond the ice to the west and northwest : but it was no small gratification that no symptom of land could be discerned in those directions. The latitude of this spot was ascertained to be $73°$ $33'$, and its longitude $88°$ $18'$: the variation $115°$ $37'$, and the dip of the needle $87°$ $36'$. Off this point the soundings where the ships lay, $2\frac{1}{4}$ miles from the land, gave 170 fathoms on a bottom of soft mud.

From the 15th to the evening of the 18th, we were engaged in trying to discover a passage through the ice between Prince Leopold's Island and the north coast of the sound. The weather was very thick and foggy so that it was impossible to avoid many smart blows from the loose ice in our way. At midnight of the 18th, the light was still sufficient to enable us to read or write in the ship's cabin. Near the north shore the sea was clear of ice; but on Thursday the 19th, the wind and swell from the east, and the absolute inutility of the compass in a heavy fall of snow, placed the vessels in a very hazardous situation. For at 2 p. m. they were found to be so close under the land that they had no more room than was necessary to put about. The land proved to be several leagues to the eastward of our position on the 4th of the month. The ice extending in some places within three miles of the coast, we had opportunities of examining various inlets by which the land seemed to be broken into islands, and not one continued tract of country. Various parts of the coast, particularly about Cape Felfoot, displayed the horizontal strata in a very distinct manner. For this perfect regularity of the horizontal distribution is one of the characteristics of the shores, where we see no marks of those great convulsions of the earth by which the component substances, in other parts of the world, have been thrown into such apparent disorder. Maxwell Bay now lay open before us, exhibiting a number of islands and inlets in the bottom. To the head-land which forms its west point was given the name of the celebrated astronomer Herschel.

On *Saturday* the 21st, the broad opening from Baffin's Bay being perfectly free of ice, want of wind alone retarded our course to the westward. When off Cape Hurd a piece of wood, seemingly part of a boat's yard, was picked up, and occasioned no small speculation, as it denoted that we were not the first navigators in the strait. At last, however, it turned out that it had been dropt by one of our own boats when formerly on the neighbouring north coast. On the 22d we found the land falling off much to the north-west, a circumstance which gave no small encouragement to our hopes; for it had been apprehended that the coast might take just the contrary direction and come to be connected with the American lands. Here we had a clear view of an open channel of upwards of eight leagues in width, in which neither ice nor land could be seen. This opening was named Wellington's Channel, from the Master General of the Ordnance; and to that portion of the broad passage from Baffin's Bay, at the beginning of Lancaster's Sound, westward to this channel, the commander gave the name of Barrow's Strait. The island on the west side of Wellington Channel was named after Admiral Cornwallis. The opening on the south side of this island was at least 10 leagues wide, and the water, though not free from ice, seemed perfectly navigable. Our ships' companies were in the best health and spirits, and the ships themselves in excellent condition; our provisions were abundant; we had therefore, every reason to look forward to the happy prosecution of the expedition.

The rocks along the shore continued still to display a succession of horizontal strata in the lower parts, but those at the top seemed to dip a little to the westward. The general substance was limestone; but in those parts which were cleared of rubbish by the sea, some beds of beautiful marble, besides loose fragments, were displayed. The ebb-tide here came from the westward, to which direction the flood must have set. This circumstance was rather discouraging for us, as it seemed to denote that the tides regarded Baffin's Bay on the east, and not the great northern American Sea, to which we were bound, on the west. It was however, probable, that the partial settings of the tide, in a sea incumbered by numerous islands, might be more governed by their positions with respect to one another, than by the situation of the great ocean by which they were all inclosed. In the evening of the 22d we had a sight of two icebergs, objects to which we had for some time been strangers.

From the entrance of Lancaster's Sound on to the meridian of $92°$ the beginning of Wellington channel, the winds had always blown in the direction of the sound, *i.e.* E. or W. but on the 23rd, a steady breeze came away from the northward, or across the strait. This strengthened the general idea that the N. shore was composed wholly of islands loosely dispersed and at considerable intervals: the probability, therefore, was, that by holding on westwardly for some time longer, we might arrive in the open ocean. But a fog coming on in the morning of the 24th, our progress was greatly retarded, especially as the bad sailing of the Griper did not permit so much sail to be set as would have been requisite. In our course we came near a vast field of ice, about 10 miles long, on a general thickness of eight feet. In this day's run we passed two islands of some extent towards the N. shore; part of the S. shore was also visible about long. $98°$. On the 24th, the wind drawing westwardly, and the ice accumulating toward the S. shore of the strait, we worked up to windward, and came within sight of a long tract of coast on the N. The appearance of the islands and the coast is quite different from that of the lands in the eastern parts of the straits; for the surface of the former is generally low, smooth, and seemingly sandy. The depth of water agrees also with what is usually remarked on low coasts, for it was, in some places, only 34 fathoms, and the deepest did not reach to 80 fathoms.

On *Friday* the 27th, the border of the ice towards the S. coast left a broad range of open sea between it and the N. coast, and the weather was uncommonly clear and steady. As the ships might, therefore, by their difference in sailing, be liable to separation, a place of rendezvous was settled. The ice on the S. then unexpectedly turned northward, quite in to the shore of an island named after Admiral Sir Thomas Byam Martin, where a large quantity was evidently fast to the ground. All passage westward being thus cut off, we stood to the southward in search of some other opening in the ice, but in vain : we returned, therefore, towards that island in the hope of finding a passage round its N. side. In approaching it the soundings lessened gradually from 80 to 23 fathoms, within 2 miles of the shore. A boat being sent on shore from the Hecla to the E. side of the island, and a fog coming on soon after, the ship stood off and on near the place, by the guidance of the soundings, and fired guns from time to time, to direct the boat in her return from the shore. The gentlemen who landed found Byam Martin island, like the other coasts in the neighbourhood, to be low next the sea, and rise up farther back. The soil visited consisted of fine sand, which, in various places, disclosed rocks of white sandstone, very soft and brittle. The vegetation, when compared with that of the lands to the E. and S. might be considered to be abundant : moss was in considerable quantities in the low moist valleys. No snow was seen on the island, the brooks were of course dried up ; but numerous masses of ice remained attached to the beach. No animals of any kind were observed: but that the brute creation, and even the human species, visited the island, was evident. Tracks of rein-deer were seen on the sands, as also their horns and hair: the skulls of white bears were also found, and the skull of a musk-ox was brought off. About a quarter of a mile back from the shore were discovered the ruins of six huts, about 12 feet long and 8 or 10 broad ; at the end of each was a small space 3 feet square, composed of 4 flat stones set on edge. In these particulars these huts exactly resemble those of the Esquimaux, or Greenlanders, on the E. coast of Baffin's bay. The small enclosures were perhaps fire-places, or rather repositories of provision. The temperature of the sandy soil was $35°\frac{1}{2}$; that of the air, the sun being under a cloud, was $33°\frac{1}{2}$. The latitude of the place of observation was $75°, 09', 23''$, and the chronometrical long. $103°, 44', 37''$. The dip of the needle was $88° 26'$, and the variation had gone westerly round by S. $14° 10'$ beyond the meridian, or it might now be reckoned $165° 50'$ easterly. The last observation of the variation was at Cape Riley, on the N. coast, in long. $91° 48'$, when it appeared to be $129°$ westerly : since that time the Hecla must have passed over the meridian N. from the magnetic pole, or that spot in which the N. end of the needle would have pointed due S.; a spot which in our position must have been in about long. 100° W. from Greenwich on the parallel of 75°. On the top of a hill or rising ground, two miles from the landing place, a heap of stones was collected over a bottle containing a bit of paper recording the ships' names and the date of their being on the coast.

Wednesday, 1st September, the compasses were now quite useless, and for some days past the haze allowed us to judge of the sun's position only by a brightness in that quarter of the heavens where he was. Having observed the general direction of the wind from the eastward, and the respective distance and situation of the Hecla and Griper while the sun was visible, the same distance and situation were carefully maintained as long as circumstances required it. Our principal dependence, however, was on the soundings, which increased or diminished, with tolerable regularity, as we were more or less off from the land. While we were on this part of the strait, or among the islands, it was rather surprising how few animals of any kind were seen; only a few seals and gulls. Being thus compelled to desist from every attempt to push on to the westward, new experiments on the dip of the needle were made on the ice, which coincided very nearly with those made on Byam Martin's island.

At last, this morning, the 1st September, the fog was succeeded by thick snow and sleet; but a breeze springing up, and there being but little ice in the neighbourhood of the ships, preparations were made for pursuing our course. After some time we had a peep at the sun, and standing on to the westward, about 9 A.M. we found ourselves a few miles off from a low point of land, which seemed to belong to a different island.—But here I must bid you all adieu, until I shall be able to tell you something correctly on the subject.

Ever your's, &c.

LETTER VII.

My dear Thomas,   *Arctic Ocean,* 1st *October,* 1819.

Little did I or any one else in this expedition imagine, that when my last letter of the first past was concluded, we were so near the termination of our operations and researches, for probably a considerable time to come. Little did we count on being arrested by the ice in this most dismal and desolate region, and compelled to pass, in such a situation, a range of dreary helpless months, the duration, and the effects of which, no one on board, not even our Greenland mariners, could conjecture. The duration of the sun's absence in any given latitude within the Arctic circle, we could calculate; but what might be the state of the land, and especially of the sea around us, what resources, if any, could be drawn from them, how we were to occupy ourselves in a night of many weeks, how to withstand the incessant assaults of intense cold, and to guard against the consequences of a long course of inactivity on the health and spirits of all on board ; on these, and various other topics, we had conjecture alone to guide us. When our story comes to be known in Europe, some of those good-natured friends, of whom Sir Peter Teazle speaks in the School for Scandal, will be ready to comfort us with the reflection, that had we left England a little sooner in the year, had we used more strenuous exertions during our passage out, had we displayed a little more ingenuity in searching for a passage across the American Arctic seas, or a little more perseverance in contending with the obstacles which opposed themselves to our progress; had we, in fact, done any thing but what we have done, instead of freezing to death in the parallel of 75° of N. latitude, we might now be indulging the hope of basking in the genial climes of the Asiatic Pacific. That we shall convince the world that, as far as our knowledge and zeal were concerned, we have not been wanting to ourselves, is perhaps too much to be expected; that we have already convinced ourselves, and one another, is beyond a doubt. After assuring you that we all, one excepted, now possess perfect health, notwithstanding the severe labours to which every man in the expedition, none excepted, has been subjected, I will return to my usual account of our proceedings.

My last letter concluded rather abruptly, with announcing our arrival, on the 1st of September, on the eastern part of what appeared to be an island detached from any land before examined or seen ; for we had run about seven leagues to the westward, without discovering any land from the southern extremity of Byam Martin Island. The part we came upon was a low point, and standing to the S.W. for a few miles, we found ourselves at noon of Wednesday, 1st September, in N. lat. 74° 59'½, and W. long- 106° 07'½. The land, like the immediate preceding islands, was of a character wholly different from that of the coasts of the eastern parts of the strait, being low along the shore, and more elevated, but neither mountainous nor precipitous, in the interior. Little snow was observed on the land, but the sea to the southward was completely invested with ice, as far as our best glasses could penetrate. Large masses of ice are aground on the shore; but still the channel between the land and the great body of ice was open and of sufficient breadth, from one to two leagues in most places. The extent of the ice and sea to the southward we could not ascertain, for no land on that side was visible since the 24th of last month, when we were in longitude 98°. In the afternoon some small rain fell, but at midnight it was succeeded by snow. Soon afterwards we were treated with the appearance of a star, the only one we had seen for about nine weeks.

In the morning of Thursday the 2nd instant, we had foggy weather with very light winds, which not being sufficient to govern the ships, they met with several severe shocks from the floating masses of ice. Had the wind been stronger, the sea was in general so open near the land, that we could have avoided them. In the forenoon a party of officers and men from both ships went ashore, having observed the water to shoal very regularly as they approached it; the depth being 6 fathoms, half a mile from the shore. In that depth were a number of masses of ice aground, a circumstance which it struck us might, if necessary, be of great service, by placing the ships between the land and those masses, which would protect us from the pressure of the great bodies of ice out at sea. The beach was flat sand, and the general ground of the land seemed to be sandstone, not unmixed, however, with limestone. The soil a little way back from the shore was a black mould, which might, in another climate, be very productive: in the moist valleys grass and moss grew abundantly, and the grass to a good height. Several pieces of coal were picked up in walking about the island; an appearance of no small importance to those who may pass through or be detained in such a climate. Great numbers of horns of deer and musk-oxen, as well as of their footsteps, were found; showing those animals to be no strangers in the island, or at least what we took to be an island. Part of the body of a musk-ox was seen, which could not have been many months on the spot. The great white bear must also inhabit, or at least visit the island, for their skulls, as well as their tracks, were seen in several places. A number of holes were found in the dry eminences, of different sizes, some probably made by field-mice, and others by foxes. Some ptarmigans were shot, and flocks of geese and ducks, as also of snow-buntings, passed the ships from the land, as if preparing or already set out on their journey for warmer climates. Two deer were seen, but too shy to be secured; and wherever any spot of good grass or moss was met, there their marks were evident. The most curious discovery was that of the horn of a narwhal, on a rising ground above a mile from the beach; carried thither probably by some Esquimaux in their summer visits to the island. A piece of a large fir-tree was discovered almost buried in the sand, about a quarter of a mile from the shore, and

10 or 12 yards above the level of the water. The spot on which the observations were made was about 100 yards back from the shore in lat. 74°, 58', and long. 107°, 03'½. The variation was 151°, 30 easterly, or 208° 30', counted round westerly. The time of high water at full and change was probably towards 2 o'clock; the rise and fall of the tide about 5½ feet. The piece of fir-tree above mentioned, and still more, the skeleton of a whale found up from the water, could never, therefore, have been transported to their position by the tides, if they were formerly as they are now. The skeleton of the whale may have occupied its present site for many ages past. The wood has evidently been crushed by the pressure of the heavy ice. On a hill behind the place of observation, the necessary notifications of the presence of the ships was deposited in a bottle under a heap of stones.

On the 3d the great body of ice was observed to draw in towards the land; it became therefore necessary, although the wind was slack, to gain as much westing as possible; which was done with all the means at our command. I must notice the peculiar beauty of this evening, the atmosphere being without a cloud, and the air frosty. The sun set with singular splendour, and the moon soon rose in all her glory. The refraction on the horizon gave her an appearance more elliptical than circular; an accident, you know, owing to the unequal effect of the air on the rays of light.

This day and the 4th we were employed in making way to the westward, passing before several headlands and bays; one of the latter running deeper into the land than we could see, nor did it seem to be worth the time which must have been lost in exploring it. Between nine and ten at night we calculated that we were on the meridian of the 110° degree of longitude, west from Greenwich. This was a point of no small importance to all persons in the expedition; and in the outset of the voyage it was considered as no contemptible exploit to be able to reach that meridian before we should be closed in for the winter. For by arriving in that longitude, within the arctic circle, the companies of both ships became entitled to 5000l. being the reward offered by the authority of parliament to any British subjects who should accomplish it. On the following morning, Sunday the 5th, after divine service, the event was communicated by Captain Parry to the company of the Hecla; and the same notification was made to the Griper. An addition to the usual allowance of meat and beer was served out to the people at dinner; and to mark the success, the seamen of themselves gave the name of Bounty Cape to a bluff headland a little to the eastward of the meridian of 110°.

Continuing her course to the westward, the Hecla made a low

projecting point, forming the farthest extremity of a bay. This point has been named after the enterprising traveller in North America, Hearne, as it stands about north from the reported position of the mouth of Coppermine river, where he came upon the sea. The wind now blew fresh from the northward, and the ice preventing the ships from proceeding westward, they worked up into the bay just mentioned, where they anchored in seven fathoms on good holding ground of mud and sand, well sheltered from ENE. round by N. to SW. Here we cast anchor, for the first time in all the voyage since we left England, an interval of four months, and this in west longitude 110°; precisely the position pointed out for obtaining the reward of our success in the expedition. In the evening of the 5th, a party of officers from the Hecla went ashore, making a second landing on this island. The ensigns were hoisted on the ships, and formal possession was taken of the island (for such it is always considered) in the name of the British nation. Whether the acquisition may ever be of any value in a political sense may be doubted, but it will always be a memorial of the skill and enterprising spirit of the persons entrusted with the researches by which it has been acquired.

On *Monday* the 6th, the wind still blowing hard from the northward, and the ice still closing in with the projecting land to the westward of the roadstead where we lay, another boat went on shore from the Hecla for the purpose of making astronomical observations, and examining the quality and productions of the soil. It was one of the objects to bring off some of the peat discovered near a mossy lake, which would have been of the greatest service as a substitute for the pit-coal on board. The quantity, however, brought on board did not quite answer our expectations: it was of a slaty texture, but burned clear with a whitish flame. Perhaps the spot where it had been seen was not recognized. On the north side of the point where the boat landed, a harbour was found; but it was small, and at the mouth was a bar, having on it only ten feet of water at low tide. The landing point is situated in latitude 74° 47', and longitude, by the chronometers, 110° 34'.

It has just occurred to me to ask whether you are always aware of the value of degrees, minutes, seconds, &c. of latitude, in situations more or less remote from the poles or the equator. The rule for ascertaining the extent of a degree of latitude on any parallel is to state this proportion. As radius to the co-sine, or sine of the complement of the latitude, so the number of nautical, geographical, or English miles in a degree on the equator, to the number of such miles in the given latitude. By this statement you will find, that, on the parallel of 75°, a degree of latitude instead of containing 60 greographical or nautical miles, contains but a little more than one-fourth part of that number; that is 15½ geographic or nearly 18 English miles. Hence the point on which the party from the Hecla landed is situated 8·8 nautical, or nearly 10 English miles west from the meridian of 110° of westlongitude from Greenwich.

At the same point the magnetic variation was 253° 43′ westerly, or 126° 17′ easterly, and the dip of the needle 88° 30′; that is, it stood nearly vertical. The temperature indicated by Fahrenheit's thermometer was as low as 25° (7° below freezing;) but to our feelings the cold appeared much more intense.

The wind becoming moderate, and the ice drawing a little off at Cape Hearne, the ships prepared to get under way: but so tenacious was the ground that it took full two hours to raise the anchor. Turning that Cape at the distance of above a mile, in deep water, the land appeared to extend about south-west by west, and the channel between it and the main ice seemed tolerably clear of broken floating ice. Hard as the wind had lately blown, the ice was not removed more, in general, than three miles or so off from the shore; a proof that out at sea the main ice was compact and solid.

As we advanced westward we found the wind follow the coast from the eastward, a fact which promised us a favourable run: but from the mast-head we had the mortification to observe the ice closing quite in to the land at the farthest extremity of our view. The ships were, therefore, made fast to what is termed by the Greenlanders a floe, that is a large field of ice usually of great thickness, in very deep water, about 80 fathoms, about four miles out from the shore. The weather was now so dark, for several hours before and after midnight, that we were obliged to make the ships fast during that period; for the compasses were entirely useless, and the water was deep very close to the land. Still judging from what had been observed by those who were in the former voyage, September was expected to be the most proper month for prosecuting our enterprize.

In the morning of *Tuesday* the 7th, the ships made sail with an easy fair breeze; for the ice seemed to be drawing off from the land; but on coming to the point we wished to turn no opening appeared, so that we were obliged to make fast again to a floe. A boat was then sent on shore to sound round some large masses of ice which were aground near the land. The purpose of this was to know whether, in the event of the main ice closing in towards the shore, the ships might be protected by those grounded bodies of ice from the pressure. Sufficient depth of water was found within them, but not room for the ships to swing round: they were, therefore, kept in their situation at the floe. This day we saw a number of musk-oxen on the land feeding; and two white hares were shot by a party on shore.

No change promising to take place in the ice without and to the westward of the ships, we looked out for some large and massy bergs (as we still called them, though wholly unlike the prodigious ice islands met with in Baffin's Bay, &c.) to which if aground we intended to secure the ships. Such masses were found, one for the Hecla fast in twelve fathoms of water about 300 yards from the shore, and another for the Griper in ten fathoms near to the land. To these bergs, therefore, both were made fast, and there we remained for several days. While we lay there the wind blew hard off the land in the night of the 11th and morning of the 12th. The ice without us began to drift to the eastward at the rate of above a mile in the hour, carrying away with it the mass to which the Hecla had been moored. Thus she escaped great danger, perhaps complete destruction, as did also the Griper, both being defended and kept in their position by their icebergs. While we lay in this situation parties from both ships went frequently on shore in search of game; for fresh food is one of the best preservatives against scurvy at sea. The musk-ox, the rein-deer, white hares, foxes, field-mice, were seen, but too far off to be struck. A number of snow-buntings were also observed, and some grouse, partly of a whitish colour, larger than a partridge, but lighter than the common British grouse. The white hares were large, weighing in general about eight pounds. A musk-ox was shot at and probably wounded; but he escaped with greater agility than was expected from his bulk and conformation. Pieces of coal were picked up scattered over the surface of the ground; but no indications of a vein of coal were any where discovered. On the 11th a musk-ox was shot by a midshipman of the Hecla, but at too great a distance to be brought to the ship. A piece of the meat taken on board and dressed as a steak, was more agreeable than had been expected, after what was said of the rank musky smell of the animal which from it has its name.

On *Sunday* the 12th, great anxiety was felt on account of a party of six men and an officer, the Greenland master belonging to the Griper, Mr. Fyfe. Early in the morning of the 11th they had been sent out to procure musk-oxen and rein-deer, the tracks of which had been seen to the westward of the ships. They were also to penetrate 15 or 30 miles into the country, to discover, if possible, its extent to the northward. As the business was to be accomplished in a day they had provisions for one day only. Not returning as expected, three gentlemen of the ship volunteered their services to go in search of the missing party; for the weather during the night was too severe for human beings

EXPEDITION IN SEARCH OF THE MISSING PARTY.

to remain abroad unless necessity compelled them to do so. But so thick was the drifting snow that this last party also missed their way back to the ship, which they reached late at night in a very exhausted state from cold and fatigue, but without any tidings of their absent shipmates. They were directed back by seeing the rockets thrown up when it grew dark. Next morning an officer of the Griper went on shore with one of the upper masts fitted as a flag staff and a large ensign, which he placed on a commanding spot about four miles back from the coast. But so thick was the snow-drift the whole day that the project could have no good effect.

On *Monday* the 13th, early in the morning, four parties with an officer to each were dispatched in search of the unfortunate men so long absent, and of whose safety little hope could now be entertained. They carried with them a number of pikes with flags to be planted in the line of each party's march, to serve as guides to the absentees, as well as to themselves in finding their way back to the ships. On each pike was hung a bottle containing written instructions, directing the missing men to the large flag-staff, where provisions would be found. When these four parties set out the thermometer was down 4° below freezing, and the wind blew hard with continued snow and drift from the westward. No words can express the joy felt by all on board both ships when, at sun-set on the third day of absence, one of the parties was seen coming along shore from the eastward with four of the original absentees. The whole seven it seems lost their way some hours after they went ashore, and wandered about utterly ignorant of their situation, until they came up to the great flag-staff, which was mistaken for another that had been planted further east some days before. Here, therefore, the party separated. The four now returned made a fire with some gunpowder and moss in the night time, and they supported themselves upon raw wild fowl. They reached the flag-staff only a few hours after the provisions had been deposited at it. They eat some bread and drank a little rum and water, which was previously mixed. It tasted, as they said, quite insipid, just the reverse of what might have been expected from men in their circumstances. Following the instruction left at the flag-staff, they set forward for the coast, and had not gone far when they met with footsteps in the snow which guided them to the party that brought them to the ships. Judging by the reports of the returned men of the route followed by their comrades after the separation, fresh parties were preparing to explore the land to the westward. Just as these were ready to set out, another of the former exploring parties appeared from the eastward with the information that the remaining three of the missing party were on their way to the coast. It was ten at night before they were brought on board by fresh men sent to meet them, having been exposed to all the rigour of the weather and want for upwards of ninety hours. All of them had suffered severely, although in different ways, their fingers and toes in particular: but by the care employed about them on board they were all in a few days restored to health. It was a happy circumstance that our poor shipmates returned as they did: for in the night it blew very hard, and the thermometer, which had never been below 15°, fell in the morning of the 14th down to 9°: in such a case not one of the party could probably have withstood the inclemency of the weather. As they lost their way in the night of the first day of their expedition they were able to give no very satisfactory account of the country they had seen. After travelling for 16 or 18 miles the land seemed to be more fertile, or rather less barren, than on the coast, for in the moist valleys grass and moss grew in good quantities In their wanderings they saw no musk-oxen, but a number of hares and rein-deer; they also observed some other animals of the deer kind, which, from their size, they supposed to be American elks. Musk oxen were, however discovered in companies by the parties sent after the missing. These last came to a fresh-water lake, supposed to extend about two miles by one, containing fish, a kind of trout: but as this happened during their wanderings they could give no account of the situation of the lake, which might prove highly serviceable to us by supplying fresh food on board.

The sudden depression of the thermometer beforementioned on the 14th, when the highest temperature in the shade was only 17°, and the lowest 9°, introduced so material a change in the climate, that on that day our winter may be said to commence.

In the morning of the 16th a strong current was observed to set to the westward, although the gale blew fresh just in the opposite direction; and at 9 A. M. the weather being tolerably moderate, both ships got under way about two miles from the land. From five to six leagues to the westward of the station where we had been so long detained, the land ran out in a very high bold headland, where the ice stretched quite in to the shore, although the heavy north-west gales had carried it off five or six miles from the coast to the eastward. The coast being frequently intersected by ravines of great depth, the gusts of wind sent down through them allowed us to carry no more sail than was just sufficient to preserve the command of the vessels. The night threatening to be very tempestuous and the coast being so lofty over very deep water where no ice could take the ground, we were, much against our will, obliged to run back to the eastward to the lower coast where we had been defended by the grounded bergs, and where we had been rendered so uneasy by the absence of the party from the Griper. About 10 P. M. a mass of ice, aground near the Hecla, was set loose by the current, and drove her several times on a projecting piece of ice under water, or what the Greenlanders call a tongue. When there is light these tongues are easily seen, and may be avoided; but this happening in the night, the Hecla received several severe blows, as if she had struck the ground: no bad consequences, however, ensued from the accident.

On *Friday* the 17th, another attempt was made to stand to the westward, which proved equally unsuccessful, for the ice was found to be again close on the land in that direction. The ice here was of great thickness, and very heavy, similar to that found on the Greenland coast. It is therefore, perhaps, not the production of the narrow seas where we are, but comes, probably, from the open northern ocean, beyond our view. The strong setting of the waters, and the drift of the ice to the westward for several days together, we were unable to explain; but one consequence seemed to follow from it, which is, that to the westward must be a large space of open sea to receive it. In order to avail ourselves of the westerly drift of the ice, it was proposed to make the ships fast to a floating field of ice, the thickest we had ever seen, and so extended that its extremities could not be perceived from the mast-head. It was not long, however, before this vast field was observed to be not only moving quickly to the westward, but also drawing in to the land: our project was, therefore, frustrated. Thus again we were forced back to the low shore to the eastward. The weather being moderate, and indeed fine in the night, in the morning of the 18th the new, or as it is technically called, the young ice, formed so quickly round the ships as to retard, and at last entirely to stop their progress. From this circumstance it was no longer a doubt whether the winter was or was not already begun: it was consequently absolutely necessary to look out for some safe sheltered haven, before we were completely beset in the ice, in a situation the most exposed on the coast.

The great mass, or floe of ice continuing to draw closer and closer on the shore, the ships were forced very near the land, in the prospect of being crushed between the immense mass and the ice accumulated and fastened to the beach. Dropping anchor in 10 fathoms water, about 100 fathoms from the land, the ships fortunately got near to what we called a berg, but what was, in fact, a hummock, or mount, formed by the pressure of one body of ice above or below others, by the force of the current. This hummock was aground, and, lying farther out than the ships, received the first shock of the floe, about 8 in the evening. The crash produced by the collision was most tremendous, and vast masses of the floe were detached and forced up on what was originally aground. The force of the floe on the berg gradually abated; but the young, or bay ice, still pressing on the Hecla in such a way that she must inevitably fall on the shore, the necessary preparations for this awful operation were made; the rudder was raised up, the sails furled, and the yards ready to take down. Such was the desperate situation of the Hecla, and her consort the Griper was in a similar position on the opposite side of the grounded berg, which partly prevented the one from seeing the other. The Griper, from her construction, fell over considerably by the pressure of the ice; but neither ship received by any means the injury naturally to be expected, in a position where no human assistance could have been of any avail. The Hecla had been forced into less than 4 fathoms of water, within 50 feet of the beach; from which she was kept off by heaps of young ice. The Griper lost one of her boats. About 9 P.M. the ice drew off a little from the land, so as to allow both ships to get into a better situation for the night. In the morning of *Sunday* the 19th, the main ice had drifted about a mile out to sea, but the channel upon the shore was still impracticable, by the multitude of broken masses united together by the young ice. Early on the 20th the wind from the N.E. quarter opened up the channel, but the current still brought the ice westward, and a projecting point bearing on where the Griper lay, forced her to take the ground with only 7 feet of water on the inside, while she was still hard pressed by the ice without. In this state of things the best thing to be done was to place the Hecla somewhere in safety, and then to send as many hands as could be spared to assist the crew of the Griper in getting her off. But the wind continuing strong off the land, the water began to open up, and in the afternoon she got afloat without any damage, having luckily grounded at low water.

The exertions and the sufferings of all on board the ships, during these occurrences, it is impossible for me to represent: but all was performed and endured with a ready determination and activity infinitely creditable to every one. The Griper had also to contend with this peculiar difficulty, that her commander, Lieutenant Liddon, who, early in the expedition, had been afflicted with rheumatism, but recovered, was again attacked, worse than ever, in the latter part of the voyage. It was proposed to remove him to the Hecla, but to this he would not agree, and remained seated on deck during the whole of the very distressing occurrences, of which I have given you a very imperfect account.

It was now manifest to every person in the expedition, that the season was too far advanced to suffer any hope to be entertained of prosecuting the voyage with any prospect of success. The winds were boisterous, often contrary; a current of two miles per hour certainly set westward, but it was so encumbered with prodigious masses of ice, and that in many places close in with the land, that it was impossible to make any way in that direction; the coast itself was lofty, precipitous, and inaccessible; such was the intensity of the cold that young or bay ice was continually and rapidly forming round the ships, whenever the water was cleared of floes. If this should be the case a little longer it would be impossible to carry the ships into any snug situation under the land, for winter-quarters, and the coast where we now were offered not the least promise of discovering any such situation. We were now at the autumnal equinox, and the meridian altitude in our position was only 15°, or the complement of our latitude. The safety of the ships, and the health and preservation of the people on board required the most speedy measures to be taken, to place them out of hazard, as much as the region we were in would admit. For these, and I doubt not various other good reasons, which may easily escape my discernment, the commander of the expedition, with the unanimous approbation of the principal officers, determined to take the first opportunity to return to the bay we had observed, and where we first dropt anchor, a little to the westward of the meridian of lon. 110°. In that bay seemed to be the only chance we had of placing the ships in security, out of the reach of the immense floes of ice which filled the offing. In consequence of this resolution, about two in the morning of *Wednesday* the 22d, the signal was made to weigh, an operation of no small difficulty, from the frost and the quantity of ice collected round the rudder and the sides. When we came off the W. point of the bay, there the young ice was so strong as to obstruct our course, and excite apprehensions that we should not be able to gain the proper anchor-ground. At length, however, the Hecla came to anchor at 8 P.M., in 9 fathoms, bottom of mud, a little to the E. of her station before. Early in the morning of the 23d, after a night of heavy snow and wind from the northward, Captain Parry went ashore to examine a harbour in the bottom of the bay, to the northward of the ship. This harbour afforded good shelter, but it had a shallow bar across the entrance. The worst circumstance of all, however, was, that the whole inner surface was one continued body of ice from 8 to 12 inches thick, all formed since we were there on the 5th inst. An officer from the Griper having mentioned that another harbour had been found a little to the westward, in the N.W. corner of the bay, on going thither it was found to be one sheet of ice, but of only 4 or 5 inches in thickness; but in other respects the position seemed to answer perfectly to what we wanted. Making holes from time to time in the ice, for nearly a mile within the entrance, the depth of water was found to be from 4 to 5 fathoms.

Friday the 24*th.*—At 6 A. M. the ships weighed, with the wind from the northward but moderate, and the weather fine. The east point of the entrance of the harbour was low, having in front a reef of rocks nearly dry, running out three quarters of a mile ; on it were a number of masses of ice fast aground. About a mile to the south of this reef, is the opposite point of the entrance of the harbour, which is higher ground. The length of the harbour, from the south point to the bottom, is nearly three miles, on a general breadth of three quarters.

From the state of the ice it was necessary to cut a channel through it, to let the ships get into their proper place, in order to be as completely protected as possible from the drifting ice out at sea. In commencing this very laborious operation (for the extent to which it seemed to be necessary to cut the ice, could not be less than two miles and a quarter), two lines were marked out with pikes, sufficiently far asunder to admit the largest ship. Along these lines the ice was cut with a saw, worked above by two men, and the pieces in the interval, cut across from time to time, to facilitate the removal of the fragments. The wind being fresh from the northward, the seamen contrived to mount sails on the loose ice, which by that contrivance, precisely suited to the invention of seamen, was carried down the canal to the sea. This accommodation did not, however, last long, for the frost in the night blocked up the canal. The ships, however, worked up as far as it was opened. As the fragments could no longer be carried towards the sea, it became necessary to sink them under the solid floe, by the men standing on one side, and by ropes drawing them under the ice. To encourage the seamen to this business the officers set the example; some of them remaining up to their knees in the water for many hours, with the thermometer never above 16°. This work being one of absolute necessity for the security of crews and ships, it was continued on Sunday, and a little past 3 P. M. both ships were drawn along by the people to the quarter destined to be our place of abode, during the tedious dark and dreary winter we are prepared to encounter. My next communication will contain some account of our operations and occupations in this situation—a situation never before voluntarily chosen, as far as I know, by any ship or ship's company; never, certainly, for any motive such as ours. Do your best to calm the apprehensions of my mother and Mary, and comfort them with the prospect of a happy meeting, after the completion of our very interesting expedition.

Farewell, my dear brother,
&c. &c.

LETTER VIII.

Dear Brother,   *Winter Harbour*, 12*th Nov.* 1819.

My last, of the 1*st October*, would inform you of our arrival in this place in the afternoon of *Sunday* the 26*th*. Since that day our proceedings and employments have been of a description more related to quiet domestic life, than to the usual duties and labours of the seamen on a voyage. We have now been long enough in this bay to discover that, although it was fixed upon more from necessity than choice, it is, in fact, the only spot, on all the coast which we have examined, where we could have been in perfect shelter and safety. The ships are placed nearest to the west side of the bay, the Hecla, although the largest, the farthest in, about two hundred and fifty yards from the west shore, and half a mile from the bottom of the bay. The Griper lies a little farther out; but both equally well protected from the external sea and ice.

No sooner were the vessels in their place than preparations were commenced for adopting every measure requisite to secure them from danger, and to preserve and promote the health, spirits, and comfort, of every member of the expedition. The service was entirely new, and although we had in both ships a master, a mate, and several seamen, who had been long accustomed to visit the arctic seas, yet their voyages were always terminated in the course of one summer, and the ships and crews were always enabled to return home before the winter set in. Our expedition was of a very different kind. We came out with the express purpose of passing the whole winter, if necessary, in the midst of regions and climates of the nature of which no man could give any thing beyond conjectural information. We were aware that in the latitude of 75° the sun would withdraw below the horizon for three months together. We knew that, even in summer, the seas around us were covered with ice floating or aground. We knew that the summer was always far advanced, or rather near its close, before navigation, even in the open sea, was practicable. How long, however, we might be detained by the ice in the harbour—how late in the summer it might be before the straits and seas were in a navigable state, to allow us to prosecute our voyage to the westward—these, and many other matters of importance, we had no means to learn.

The first care has been to trim the ships in the way the most likely to preserve the masts, sails, and rigging. The lower masts alone to stand; only the main-top-mast of the Hecla is retained, for the purpose of making experiments on atmospherical electricity, and for hoisting a flag for the direction of shooting or other parties on land. The lower yards have been secured fore and aft, to support the frame of the housing or roof over the ships, constructed of planks covered with strong cloth, such as in waggon tilts. The boats, ropes, sails, and every thing that could take up room on the upper decks, have been carried on shore and covered with canvas. Being there in a very cold freezing temperature, the sails and ropes are perfectly safe, whereas in the ship they would be thawed but never dried, and would, of course, be rotted. To secure the ships against the breaking up of the ice, anchors were carried and fastened on the land. The next operation regarded the accommodation of the officers and men on board, in which every contrivance, that experience and anxious care to preserve them all in health and spirits could suggest, was carried into effect. But of these the details would be of very little service to an inhabitant of the genial climes of England, especially to one who never slept a night on board ship. It is, to be sure, a circumstance peculiarly encouraging to us that, with the unfortunate exception of the commander of the Griper, not a single person is now on the sick list. From cold and wet a few slight complaints have occasionally appeared; but they have been easily removed. Scurvy, the dreadful scourge of mariners in long voyages and cold weather, without the means of procuring fresh provisions or vegetable diet, is hitherto unknown. Every preventive which could be devised, was liberally put on board before we sailed. The ships' companies are now, therefore, in fact, in as good condition as when we left England. Various expedients have been adopted to keep the beds and bed-places dry and warm, an operation of very difficult execution, where a number of human bodies are collected together. What can be done, however, will certainty not be neglected. Although a large quantity of coal was laid in for both ships, yet, as we have hitherto discovered no fuel of any kind, on which dependence can be placed in case of need, economy in firing becomes of the strictest rigour; and, in this article alone, do we feel any restraint. By exercise, however, and habit, we hope to think less in future of this privation, of the necessity of which all of us are thoroughly convinced. The seamen and marines were distributed into small divisions, each under an officer, who was accountable for the orderly, clean, and neat appearance of his men, who were strictly inspected by the commander of the ships morning and evening, as were their bedplaces, while they were upon deck. The greatest obstacle to comfort was, that it was next to impossible to dry any wet clothes in the open air, where they froze and became moist again when carried into the warmer atmosphere between decks, where we were obliged to hang them on lines. A considerable supply of Donkin's preserved meat, of concentrated vegetable soup, vinegar, lime-juice, wine, beer, &c. furnished the means of varying the provisions served out for the ship's company; and whenever any game has been procured, it has been divided, without the smallest distinction of quality or quantity, among officers and men. Our bread is baked on board instead of bringing out biscuit.

To give you, my dear Thomas, some notion of the manner in which our time on board is usually employed, you must know that the day and night are each divided into four watches of three hours each. At six in the morning the men are called up, and the decks are cleaned with warm sand. At eight all go to breakfast, and at a quarter past nine the men are inspected on deck. While the examination is going on below, the men have a run on deck. They are then, if the weather permit, sent to take exercise on shore till noon, when they dine. In bad weather they walk or run, or dance on deck, keeping time to an organ, or to their own song; the officers exercise themselves also on shore, from noon till two when they go to dinner. The danger of snow-drifts however confines these excursions to narrow bounds. In the afternoon the men are employed below in various ways, preparing articles necessary for the ship. At six P. M. they are again inspected and go to supper, after which they amuse themselves in any way they choose, at various games, dancing, singing, on the lower deck till nine, when they go to bed, and their lights are extinguished. The officers have tea while the men are at supper, and in reading or writing, conversation, a game at chess, a tune on the violin or the flute, pass the time till half-past ten, when all not on duty retire to rest.

To guard against the danger from fire, proper officers visit the lower deck every half hour; and large holes are opened twice a day, close by the ship's sides, to obtain water. On Sundays divine service is performed in both ships, and a sermon read; and you can not conceive with what propriety and decorum it is attended by every man of the crew.

When the ships were properly arranged, and the system of discipline and economy was established, a plan was pitched upon for establishing an observatory. The spot was nearly half a mile to the westward of the ships, and a wooden building was erected on a more sheltered position, to hold the astronomical clocks and other instruments. So hard frozen was the ground that it was with great difficulty holes could be made, to fix the posts of the house, which was framed of double planks, with a stuffing of moss; so that it is hoped a stove may be able to keep it in an equable temperature for the use of the clocks, &c. The observatory is in N. Lat. 74° 47′ 10″, and W. Long. 110° 48′ 15″.

It was a happy circumstance that we gained this harbour when we did; for on that very night, the 26th September, the thermometer fell to 1° below zero on the beginning of the scale, although the wind was NNW off the land, and the weather was moderate and fine. The day before it fell only to 7° and the day after to 5° both above zero.

In the morning of the 27th the sea, as far as could be seen from a neighbouring hill, exhibited one continued frozen mass, without a single perceptible spot of open water. The land around us presented also a dreary scene, being every where coated with snow of different depths as it was drifted by the wind.

A week after our arrival we had a trial, and a satisfactory one it was, of the excellence of the station we had found for the ships; for a heavy gale coming on from the southward, the external ice was found to have squeezed up the ice at the mouth of our harbour, while that within remained solid, and the vessels wholly unaffected.

We had not been long in our winter quarters when we began to have sight, if not visits, of several animals inhabitants, for a time at least, of the island. On the 1st of this month one of the artillery-men on board being on shore, was followed by a formidable white bear over the ice up to the Hecla, from which several shots were fired, and he was certainly wounded, but he escaped. That he was struck was evident from the blood which stained his fur. Being pursued by a party over the ice, he slipped out of their hands by swimming over a narrow opening of water near the land, where he soon again began to change his white colour in consequence of his wounds. Skulls and other parts of the white bear have been found in the island; but this was the first living animal of that kind, and a noble formidable animal he really was, that has come within our view in this quarter. The white fur of this bear was remarkable, when it is considered that it was contrasted with the snow on the ground; for I am told that in general it has a faint yellowish tinge: perhaps he was very young, although of a large size.

On the same day some of the people had the good fortune to shoot a rein-deer, all white excepting a brown spot toward the tail. The carcass without the skin weighed nearly 150 pounds. On the 10th a herd of deer were seen on the shore, and a party went after them. One was shot, and another wounded, but he made off. In pursuing him eagerly (for fresh meat is no doubt to people in our situation an acquisition of great value) the party were drawn to a considerable distance; so that they could not get back to the ships in proper time to comply with an order from the commander, that every person without exception should always be on board before sun-set. One man who had separated from the rest and came in about 7 P. M., had his hands frost-bitten, and was otherwise so benumbed and stupified by the cold that he could give no distinct account of his companion still on the land. Poles with lanterns were planted on the heights round the harhour, guns were fired from the ships, and rockets discharged. At last, near midnight, the missing man came on board; and to our surprise did not appear to suffer in any way from the cold, although he had been so much longer in it. In consequence of this accident a fresh and a very proper order was issued, to compel the men to attend to the former; which was, that all the expense incurred in rockets, firing, or other methods for their restoration, should be charged to the persons who occasioned it, by not being on board by sun-set.

The effects of intense cold on the human frame, mind as well as body, are strikingly powerful. Some of our young gentlemen of the above party, when conducted into the cabin to the commander, had every symptom of inebriation, a thing impossible in their case: but as bodily warmth was restored they gradually returned to the proper use of their faculties, and were able to give distinct information of their proceedings. For it is not merely the severe cold that confounds the people on the land, but the drifting of the snow, which, being always in a loose frozen state, is driven about by the wind in such a manner that a person is unable to keep his eyes open, and of course loses his way.

The aurora borealis, northern lights, or streamers, as they are often called, were seen in the evening of the 13th, but only as a pale whitish light in the west near the horizon; so that we have been disappointed in the hope of beholding that striking natural phenomenon in greater perfection as we approached to the north pole. On the following day a wolf appeared at a good distance from the ships. His colour was white, but in other respects he resembled the Greenland dog. On *Friday* the 15th, we were compelled to give up all hope of obtaining wild-fowl, for on that day the ptarmigans appeared in covey for the last time. On the same day a herd of fifteen rein-deer were seen: but none of them were killed, for the weather being clear, in a country perfectly destitute of cover, it was impossible to get near them. It was found also, that from the moisture which freezes on the lock, from the breath or other causes, the piece frequently misses fire. The deer were all lying on the ground when first seen, excepting one, perhaps a stag, who showed great anxiety to quicken their flight, going round them and pushing them on with his horns. At this time, although the heavens were quite clear over head, so thick was the snow-drift along the surface of the ice, as well as the land, that it was necessary to extend a small rope between the two ships, to guide those who had occasion to pass from the one to the other, although it was only about 120 yards.

On *Saturday*, the 16th of *October*, was the last opportunity we had of observing the sun's meridian altitude, although he still continued to rise above our horizon for some time afterwards On the 18th, the parties in quest of game on shore, found the deer collected together in large bodies, as if arranging matters for leaving the island, and migrating to the American continent to pass the severity of the winter: for after this time very few were ever seen. Their removal was a clear proof that the seas and channels to the southward of our station are completely frozen over. One deer was shot this day, and it has been several times remarked, that all the deer seen in this quarter seem to be travelling westward, and they always make off in that direction when pursued. Whether this ought to be considered as indicating the existence of land in that direction, in which they can exist more conveniently than here in winter, or by which they can better pass over to America, it is impossible to say: but the fact deserves notice. For some days past parties have been employed in digging moss-peat for fuel; but we find it difficult to dry it for use.

The ships have now for some time been as completely united with the ice in the harbour as if they were a part of it. Apprehensions begin to be entertained that, in the case of the ice being pushed above its present level by any change out at sea, the vessels may be exposed to danger. It has, therefore, been considered whether it would not be best to cut away the ice round the ships, to allow them to rest wholly on the water below. But even at spring tides in WINTER HARBOUR, (for that is the name by which we distinguish our present quarters, a circumstance I ought to have sooner mentioned) the difference between high, and low water is only a little more than 4 feet. It has also been remarked that at full tide the whole sheet of ice separates from the shore, raising and sinking the ships along with it, which, of course, are not exposed to any strain by the motion. It was also feared that the ice, by pressure on the ship's sides, might start a plank or otherwise injure them, but it may be doubted whether such lateral pressure exists. Water, we know, expands in the act of freezing; but ice, once fully formed, is subject to no more enlargement, and consequently can exert no pressure. As, however, no possible harm could result from cutting away the ice adhering to the ships, the crews were employed for two days in the operation; for the ice was within a trifle of 2 feet in thickness: this is to be repeated every day.

We are now and then visited by a wolf, or a white fox; but

unless we can entrap them, our acquaintance does not promise to be very intimate. The animals are very shy, and we have no way of getting near them unseen, even if we could depend on our arms going off. They are probably attracted round the ships by the scent of what refuse of the provisions may be thrown out on the ice.—Just as I have said : a fox has been caught in a trap made of an empty cask, having at one end a bait fastened to a slide at the opposite open end ; so that when the bait was touched down went the slide, and master Reynard was fairly caught without a hair being hurt. He is entirely white, and about the size of a good hare, but his long brush makes him appear much larger. *Ce n'est pas l'habit qui fait le moine,* as the French say. It is not the dress that makes the monk. Notwithstanding the emblematic purity of our fox's habiliments, he is just as much a fox in his heart as ever a brown gentleman caught in Yorkshire. When discovered in the cask and taken out, which he suffered to be done without resistance, he closed his eyes, stretched himself out, and remained motionless ; expecting no doubt to disarm the attention of his surrounding foes, as if already dead, and then quickly make off. But the biped will prove too wily for the quadruped, who may perhaps learn to accommodate himself to our ways, and pay a visit to Old England.

Wednesday, the 20th, we had a proof of the remark that positive cold, unaccompanied by moisture and wind, is much more tolerable than might be expected, from observing the state of the thermometer. On that day the instrument continued steady at 15° or 16° below zero : but as far as bodily sensations were concerned, the weather being clear and calm, was really pleasant.

On the same day, our hunting, or rather shooting parties returned to the ships, with the mortifying information that not a single animal of game or of prey had been seen, although all the usual sporting ground had been explored to a considerable extent of country. Our hopes, therefore, of varying a little our usual fare, are nearly dissipated.

In the evening, the aurora borealis again displayed its wonders, in a broad bow of whitish light from NNW to SSE. the centre of the arch being on the E. side of the zenith. The brightest part was in the south, from which the light darted frequently upwards. No effect seemed to be produced by the aurora on the magnetic needle. On the following day, a little before sun-set, that is before three P. M. the weather very clear, a halo or circle with the colours of the rainbow was seen round the sun, at a considerable distance from his body. The circles, and mock-suns, and mock-moons, as they are vulgarly called, are by no means rare, as I understand, in these northern climates : should any one of a kind more remarkable than another appear while we are here, you shall have an account of it.

As October drew to a close, and the sun was preparing to leave us, the appearance of the heavens at his rising and setting was singularly beautiful: a rich bluish purple bordering the horizon and gradually passing into a deep red above. Such was the mildness (that is to say what we reckon mildness) of the weather at the same time, that the thermometer which on the 22d stood at 3° below zero, rose on the 23d, to 6°, on the 24th, to 1°, on the 25th, to 5°, on the 26th, to 4°, all above zero, and again on the 27th fell down to 4° below zero. It was also observed that, on deck and the outside of the Hecla, the temperature was always from 2° to 5° and and even 7° higher than on the beach; an effect produced doubtless by the comparative warmth arising from the fires and the people on board. In the last three days of the month the thermometer sunk to 28° below zero: but in the course of the 31st, it remained for some time at only 4° below that point. During all these days we had only light breezes off the land, and generally fine weather. It has been frequently, indeed I may say constantly remarked, that when the wind blows from the northwards no particular coldness is indicated by the thermometer more than in winds from the opposite quarter. When it blows fresh, however, from any point of the compass, the thermometer always rises or indicates an increased temperature; although at that very time the cold, if we judge by our feelings when exposed to the wind, appears much more intense than in calm weather, even with a lower indication of the thermometer. If in the course of our observations we discover any fixed correspondence between the rise and fall of the instrument, and the strength or feebleness of the wind, you shall be informed of our discoveries.

By being exposed for a course of months to the variations, and often to the intense severity of the northern and arctic climates, our bodies have, by a happy fitness of structure and susceptibility, become so far habituated to the state of the atmosphere, that it appears to me, and to others also, like a dream, to find that we can, without serious inconvenience, perform all necessary operations in the open air, whilst the thermometer indicates a temperature of which in England you can have no experience. I remember to have read, some years ago, of experiments of a contrary nature made in London, by several scientific persons, in the view of discovering how high a degree of artificial heat they could sustain. The results I do not now recollect, but the thermometrical degree was greatly above what could be supposed. To whatever extent human beings and other animals may possess this power of adaptation, not so is it with metallic bodies; for we always found them to assimilate themselves precisely to the temperature in which they were placed. Hence has arisen one of the greatest obstacles we have met with in performing astronomical and geographical observations. The instruments being constructed of brass, that they may not be acted upon by the magnetic power, have often become so cold that it becomes highly painful to handle them. As the winter advances the cold will, no doubt, become more and more intense: it will then, it is to be feared, be in some cases impossible to use some of our most valuable instruments in the open air, where alone they can be used. The sensation produced by handling metals in the open air is similar to that excited by the opposite extreme of heat, and the skin is affected and even taken off in the same manner as by burning. One proof of the intense cold communicated to the metallic instruments by the open air is this, that when they are carried into the warmer atmosphere of the cabin, the moist vapour there is instantly condensed round the instruments, and covers them with a coating of ice, which again thaws as the metal acquires the temperature of the cabin.

The sun having for some time been drawing nearer and nearer to the day of his departure for three months to come, at last, on Thursday, the fourth of November, he was, according to the almanack, to take his dreaded leave, and consign us over to a long and melancholy night. But the invidious atmosphere was so obscured by clouds, that even those who mounted to the top of the nearest hill were not permitted to take a parting look of the mariner's best and truest friend and conductor in his wanderings over the pathless deep. By comparing the instant of his actual disappearance below the horizon with the instant of his astronomical disappearance, information might have been obtained respecting the refracting power of the atmosphere on the meridian in a very low temperature. Of this power a curious instance occurred just a week afterwards; for an officer of the Hecla having gone up to the mast-head from curiosity, there perceived nearly one half of the sun's body above the horizon. In this case the elevation produced by the refraction must have been at least two degrees.

The day after the sun left us, the temperature of the air (I need not add in the shade, for we are always now in the shade) was 16°, or 16 degrees below zero on Fahrenheit's scale; that of the water at the surface was $+ 28°$, or 28 degrees above zero, and that of the water, at the depth of five fathoms under the ice, was as high as $+ 30°$. The specific gravity of the water at the surface, at a temperature of 52°, was 1·0204.

Experiments were made at the same time to ascertain the electric state of the atmosphere, both when clear and when clouded, and even during a display of the aurora borealis; but always without any effect. The chain employed to attract the electric matter was hoisted up above the head of the Hecla's main-top-mast (which, as I formerly mentioned, was retained in its place for that and other purposes when the ships were dismantled), and the lower end carried clear of the ship and rigging down to the ice on the outside.

We are now firmly installed in our winter-quarters for a long time to come, in which little variety of importance can be looked for in the transactions or occurrences of our secluded little society. I must, therefore, lay aside my pen for the present, to resume it occasionally, as matter may present itself, from which information or amusement may be collected. Health and comfort to all at home.

Ever your's, most truly,
&c. &c.

LETTER IX.

My dear Brother,
Winter Harbour, 1st Jan. 1820.

You will not question my sincerity when I declare, that the greatest hardship we experience in this expedition, particularly since we have been fast beset in the ice, arises from our inability to relieve our relations and friends from their anxious apprehensions and forebodings, on the subject of our mode of existence, and even of our existence itself in any way.

But, believe me, such imaginations are not confined to your happy side of the Atlantic. We, also, in spite of our indispensable occupations, find abundance of time to conjecture, how you may all have passed these nine eventful months since we put to sea. I left you all in that most desirable situation which results from good health, equable spirits, commendable pursuits, encouraging prospects, easy circumstances, and moderate wishes. The happiness accruing from such a combination I have too often witnessed to have any doubt of its permanency. But accidents may happen, changes may supervene; my mother's affectionate anxiety for her first-born may impair her usual good constitution; Mary is but delicate; you yourself may draw too freely on your fund of animation and vigour;—thus, at times, I indulge my *mays*, until, copying from the practical philosophy of honest Sancho, I am ready to exclaim, Body of me! things are not half so bad as all this comes to.

My last letter brought us down to the 12th of *November;* since which time, to say the truth, few things have occurred among us worthy to be recorded, excepting in a regular ship's journal, where every thing ought to be recorded, of negative as well as positive importance. You have heard our worthy father tell the story of a person, with whom he was a little acquainted, who had been for some years a diplomatic agent, resident at a German court of the second or third order. Returning to London on leave of absence, and presenting himself before the Secretary of State for Foreign Affairs, " How came it about, pray Mr. —— (said the Minister), that, for a very considerable period I had no communication of any kind from your hand ?" " Why, Sir, there was nothing really going on at —— which deserved to be communicated to you." " That is precisely the thing which, for a long time past, I wished to know."

I cannot, however, suffer this opening of the new year to pass over without, in the old-fashioned way, wishing you all at home, and all inquiring friends abroad, many happy returns of the season. We also augur to ourselves no small encouragement and success, for we have now weathered, as we say, the shortest day; and when things, you know, have passed the worst, they must necessarily mend.

Nothing is more sure than the remark, that if you do not find employment or amusement for people, they will find for themselves. This remark is most commonly applied to children, but the sapient remarkers might, with a little self-examination, apply it to themselves. We have, indeed, no children among us; but a true seaman, excepting in what relates to his own peculiar duties, is really no wiser, no more considerate, than a very child. In a former communication I gave a general account of the system of occupation and discipline introduced by our commander among the ships' companies, to be adhered to so long as the presence of the sun, and the temperature of the weather, should render it practicable. But, since we have been shrouded in darkness, since our day has been turned into uninterrupted night, since the whole round of the seaman's duties have been brought to a termination ; for now he can, as we say, neither hand, reef, splice, nor steer ; various projects have been canvassed to discover entertainment as well as employment for our grown children of the forecastle. And, to tell you the truth, the gentlemen of the quarter-deck were not less glad to devise some method to vary the monotony of their official life, in which astronomical and meteorogical observations promised to be their principal avocations. Excursions on shore were no longer to be practised ; the geology of the country seemed to offer little of interest either of utility or rarity; the animal world had nearly all forsaken us; and the officer's charge was now become almost a sinecure.

Idleness is equally injurious to the mind and the body; and, in our position, could not fail to induce, or at least to dispose for disease. Two schemes were therefore proposed, and unanimously adopted. The one, to fit up a sort of theatre, on which to represent such little pieces as might interest and amuse the men: the other, to establish a sort of weekly newspaper, to be supported by the voluntary contributions (literary that is to say) of the officers of both ships. Of this work, Captain Sabine, of the Royal Artillery, the astronomer of the expedition, was to be the conductor or editor. The theatricals were placed under the superintendance of Lieutenant Beechey, as stage-manager; the commander himself, Captain Parry (for so I designate him, although he has only the rank of Lieutenant in the Navy), took his share in the common effort to excite and maintain cheerfulness and good-humour, excellent preservatives of health, spirits, contentment, and comfort, among the men.

Monday, the 1st of *November*, 1819, will ever be memorable in the history of literature. On that day appeared, composed, edited, but not printed, within the arctic circle, within fifteen degrees of the North Pole of the earth, the first number of the " North Georgian Gazette, or Winter Chronicle;"—a work, take it all in all, without a fellow. In assembling matter for this work, you Londoners, more embarrassed by the multiplicity than by the scarcity of news, next to the sirloin John Bull's choicest treat, will be puzzled to imagine what the contributors had or could find to say. But what with the knowledge of some, the invention of others, the criticisms of a third order, the enterprize has never once been suspended for lack of matter. The experiment was, you may suppose, a little hazardous: the *genus irritabile* comprises many a scribbler besides the poet. But whether it is to be ascribed to the good sense and moderation of the writers, to their feeling of the propriety of the undertaking, to the chilling freezing powers of the climate, the only thing worth notice is this, that up to this day the " Arctic Miscellany" seems fully to produce the intended effect.

Preparations having been made on board the Hecla, our new theatre was opened on *Friday*, the 5th of *November*, with the popular piece of " Miss in her Teens." Fitted up on the quarter-deck, where the companies of both ships were accommodated; for the distance between them did not exceed half a cable's length, or sixty fathoms, and a line was extended between them, as I said before, to guide those who passed backwards and forwards; the performance afforded a rich treat to our poor fellows, who felt most thankful for the pains taken by their officers to promote their entertainment, and thereby shorten their dreary days. The exhibition lasted two hours, and seemed to answer so well the intended purpose on its first appearance, that it was resolved to repeat it once every fortnight. The delight of the crews was not, however, limited to the mere hours of performance: several cheerful days of anticipation and recollection were employed in fitting up and taking down the theatre, the only structure of the kind probably ever erected on the parallel of 75° north, and in a temperature at the beginning of Fahrenheit's scale, on the outside of the ship, and at the freezing point on the inside, close to the stage. The house was opened with an appropriate address, composed and delivered by Mr. Wakeham, clerk of the Griper, who also furnished two songs that were sung between the acts. Not the least amusing part of the business was to hear the judgments passed on the entertainment by our honest tars, who wanted terms to express their gratification, until the boatswain, a very formidable personage I assure you, on board ship, helped them out by informing them, that fine, excellent, and other epithets they had employed were nothing to the purpose; for what they had heard and seen was, " in fact, real true philosophy."

Although we were deserted by every animal from which we could have drawn any benefit about the time when the sun disappeared, yet the wolves were more faithful. Them we heard prowling and howling about on the edge of the ice in the dark, and, on some occasions, they ventured very near the ships, where by their scent they, no doubt, expected to appease their famished maws. It was curious to observe, at those times, the terror which agitated our pretty little white fox, when he heard their too well known voice. None of our people were ever attacked by the wolf, who, on the contrary, seemed very shy and unwilling to let them get near him. A wolf, however, once gave chase to one of our dogs, pursuing him until he took refuge near the ship with the people he accompanied. While the dog was trotting on towards him, the wolf remained still in his place; but when he saw the dog halt, and draw no nearer, then he sprung forward at full speed. Had the dog been far from protection, the wolf would soon have overtaken him.

It was already mentioned that it was deemed prudent to cut open the ice daily round the ships' sides. In the third week of November so rapidly did it form in the opening that it required the labour of several hours every day to keep it clear. This labour would now, as the frost became more and more intense, continually increase; and the men's exposure to cold and wet could not fail to endanger their health; orders were consequently given to intermit the business until the severest part of the season should be gone past. The ice generally formed to the thickness of four or five inches, and once to above seven in 24 hours; the air being at 12° below zero. To give you some notion of the quantity of light afforded by the sun's beams reflected from the atmosphere, at noon on the 17th, when he was nearest to our southern horizon, I have to tell you that then, for the first time, we saw *Capella*, a star of the first magnitude; and half an hour afterwards the stars of the second magnitude in the Great Bear were also visible. In the afternoon of the same day, about 3 o'clock we were treated with the view of a very singular aurora borealis, when the sun was only about 5° below the horizon : it lasted about half an hour. To give an accurate description of this phenomenon, or indeed of any aurora, which as you have sometimes seen, is continually shifting its place and its appearance, is impossible : I can only say that, from the rapid darting and flashing of the light behind a dark cloud, it had a striking resemblance to the explosion of a magazine, or other vast mass of gunpowder.

The cold now increased rapidly within the ships, while the wind brought a heavy snow-drift off the land to the northward. The vapour arising from the men's breath, or other causes, in the sleeping places in the night, immediately froze to the timber-works; and it required some hours' labour to collect and remove the ice. While it remained congealed it did no great harm; but the warmth of the fires, and even of the men, in the night-time, thawed it so much as to render the bed-places very damp; an accident which must, in time, be very prejudicial to their health : nor was it easy to contrive the means of preventing it. Another effect of the severe cold was, that any hurt received by the men, or frost-bite, became very obstinate in resisting the means of cure.

It was formerly remarked that the mercury in the tube of the thermometer always rose while the wind blew strong, from whatever quarter it came ; although it was always at that very juncture that, to our feelings, the temperature was the lowest. Of this a remarkable instance occurred early in what might be called the morning of Sunday the 21st. The mercury rose from $-46°$ at midnight to $-40°\frac{1}{2}$ at 3 A. M. when a gale began from the land. It continued to blow hard, and the mercury to rise till the following midnight, when it stood at $-21°$. This gale was accompanied by a drift of snow so furious, that it was impossible to leave our shelter in the ships, for the two following days. During this time the temperature, down in the ships holds, varied between 27° and 34°, and, which was remarkable, the after hold, although the most remote from the fires, was always the warmest. For I must mention that very moderate fires were kept up in the Captain's cabin. A considerable portion of our beer was frozen in the casks, and on the lower deck the heat was seldom higher than 40° in the day, that is only 8° above the freezing point of water.

Wednesday 24th, another play was brought out to the great delight of the men, who had talked of little else since our last performance. The three last nights of the month were employed in lunar observations, that is in measuring the angular distance between the moon and certain fixed stars, for the purpose of calculating the Longitude of our position, by observing the difference in time between the positions of those bodies as indicated by our chronometers, and as computed for the observatory of Greenwich. During this course of observations, the mercury was never higher than —34°; yet, while the weather was calm, no material inconvenience was felt from even that intense cold. On the 29th, a very remarkable fact occurred; the mercury employed in forming an artificial horizon for the lunar observations, was found congealed and solid after exposure for several hours to a temperature never beyond 36° below zero. Now it is known that pure mercury retains its fluidity down to the 40th degree below zero; the congelation at —36°, therefore, must have been produced by some impurity in the mercury, perhaps from its combination with a portion of the lead of the cistern or vessel in which it was placed. That the temperature on this occasion was not in fact lower than 36_0 was proved by another mercurial thermometer, which retained its fluidity and indicated the same temperature.

Wednesday, 1st December, a portion of a halo or circle was seen round the moon then near the full. The diameter of the halo was about 16°. Part of a horizontal circle or plane of white light passed through the moon, and at the points where it crossed the halo two paraselenae or mock-moons appeared with prismatic colours. Immediately over and under the moon in the halo were other bright spots, particularly that above her. Similar phenomena presented themselves round the moon about the same hour in the following evening. The weather on both occasions was fine but a little hazy. Some days afterwards a small meteor or shooting star fell in a northwest direction: it resembled one observed on the 28th of the preceding month. The weather about this time became so mild as to occasion considerable inconvenience in the ships, by thawing the ice formed between decks: but when the thermometer again sunk 15° or 20° below zero, the ice became solid and the inconvenience disappeared.

I intended to communicate to you some particulars respecting our little arctic fox, but he has left us, his chain having got loose. He was seen on the following day, and the mark of the chain has been seen on the snow. But the poor creature must soon fall a prey to some wolf, or be starved, for with it he can neither escape from his enemies, nor dig out the field-mice, which are probably his chief food. While in the ship he became daily more tame, and might be handled without danger. He would eat whatever was given to him, but his chief food consisted of bread and peas.

The aurora borealis and gleams of light, seeming to proceed from behind dark clouds, have been several times seen of late. From the 10th to the 20th of the month the thermometer stood uncommonly high, and on *Friday* the 17th, at 4 P. M. the mercury rose to zero, the beginning of the scale, a point which it had never reached since the beginning of November. The wind was strong with heavy drift of snow. Notwithstanding the fires and the number of people on board the ships, the pump-wells were completely frozen, so that the pumps could no longer be used ; nor could the ice, which was 20 inches in thickness, be removed without endangering them. Fortunately, however, the cold and the tightness of the vessels prevented any considerable increase of water in the hold. The frost, however, produced another effect of more importance in the prosecution of our voyage, by bursting some of the bottles containing our stock of lemon juice. The contents became quite solid with the exception of a small quantity of acid highly concentrated in the middle of the frozen mass, which when thawed tasted almost like water. The cases of bottles which were nearest the ship's sides suffered the most. The vinegar also froze in the casks, and when thawed was nearly insipid. On the contrary, a small quantity of highly concentrated vinegar, taken on board for an experiment, and which was sufficiently acid for use when diluted with five or six times its quantity of water, remain unaffected. At the temperature of 25° below zero it thickened like honey, but never froze so as to burst the vessel containing it. By the use of this vinegar much room would also be saved in the hold ; the lemon juice for voyages in these climates ought also to be highly concentrated.

The aspect of the objects around us is now most dismal : the death-like silence is interrupted only by the bellowing of the winds or the howling of the wolves. The aurora borealis itself, however curious, is not to be compared, for brilliancy and beauty with those seen in the Shetland and Orkney isles, or in the Atlantic ocean in similar latitude. Our plays and other amusements have however still maintained the men in cheerfulness and good spirits : and our newspaper has afforded employment occasionally for several of the higher class.

Tuesday the 21st of *December*, the shortest day in the year, as you Britons would reckon it, brought to us this consolation, that we had at last attained the middle of our long and dreary night. The sun set for us on the 4th of November : we ought, therefore, to look for his rising again about the 8th of February next; our winter's night will thus comprehend ninety-six of your nights and days, of four and twenty hours together. Tedious, melancholy as this period might appear to us, accustomed to a very different distribution of the year and of time ; no less true is it that what with necessary occupations connected with the expedition, what with voluntary employment, what with the amusements naturally suggested by our situation, this first half of our winter has passed away with unexpected velocity. So true is this that, it in some measure required a consultation of the almanack to persuade some, if not all of us, that we were already arrived at that point of our orbit round the sun, in which he is the farthest below our horizon. It was a subject of no little consideration, among the principal officers of the expedition, to devise methods of employing the men in some healthful and useful way, during a period in which the ordinary occupations of seamen could neither be required, nor indeed be practicable. Judge, then, with what satisfaction the commander learned, that the ships' companies secretly complained that they were so constantly employed by his orders as to have no time to attend to their own personal concerns. To this judicious arrangement and intermixture of easy labour and cheerful relaxation must, in a great degree, be ascribed the singularly healthy condition in which the crews of both ships were maintained, during our imprisonment.

At noon every day, when the atmosphere was clear, after the sun ceased to appear above the horizon, twilight was sensibly perceived; even on the shortest day we had light enough to take, for an hour or two, the exercise of walking on shore, or on the ice. The reflection of this light from the snow, joined to the occasional brightness of the moon, prevented us, even in the most tempestuous weather, from being involved in that blackness of darkness so frequent in more southern climates. By holding the book to the south at noon, in clear weather, one might read the print of a small pocket prayer-book. To prevent any encroachment on the regular order of discipline established by the commander of the expedition, great care was taken that the various periods fixed for rising and going to bed, for meals, occupation, exercise, amusement, &c. should be strictly adhered to, in the same manner as when the sun was visible. By a little practice the strangeness of some of these employments of the day, being discharged in what, to all intents and purposes, was night, was entirely effaced.

Saturday the 25th, being Christmas day, it was celebrated with all due solemnity. Divine service was performed in the morning on board both ships, and an addition was made to the usual allowance of fresh meat for the men. The officers had also their social meal; a piece of English beef was roasted on the occasion, which had been preserved in perfect order from the preceding May, without salt, solely by the cold of the climate to which we had ever since been exposed. The thermometer this day, when at the maximum, was at $-24°$, the barometer mean 29·648 inches. The wind being from the N.W., but very moderate, and the weather fine, several officers had a pleasant walk on shore for an hour.

About 8 A.M. of the 26th, it blew a fresh breeze from the same quarter, and the thermometer rose as usual from $-20°$ to $-6°$: but towards midnight the mercury fell to $-17°$. Continuing to sink for the four ensuing days, on the 30th it had sunk to $-43°$, a point to which we had never before seen it descend. The weather during these four days was very calm, clear, and fine. Between 7 and 8 A.M. of the 30th, the barometer rose to 30·75 inches, a height to which it had never before risen since we left the Thames. The heavens to the S. at noon, near the horizon, displayed all the colours of the rainbow.

Having now brought down our transactions and observations to the close of 1819, I will also close this rambling epistle, with expressing every good wish for all at home, and all their and my good friends.

Your's most affectionately,
&c. &c.

LETTER X.

Winter Harbour, 1st *March,* 1820.

DEAR BROTHER,

I AM no poet, you know, nor do I pretend to be a judge of poetry; but there are certain energetic productions which early made an impression on my memory;—an impression not soon, I trust, to be effaced. In Paradise Lost, for instance, I have often been struck with the skill displayed by Milton in forming the character of the arch fiend, in which envy and malice, too often, I fear, the companions of state-ambition, are the prominent features. After a voyage still more extraordinary than ours, the infernal hero, landing on the verge of the solar system, thus addresses the life and soul of that system " which now sat high in his meridian power."

> " O thou that with surpassing glory crown'd,
> Look'st from thy sole dominion like the god
> Of this new world; at whose sight all the stars
> Hide their diminished heads; to thee I call,
> But with no friendly voice, and add thy name,
> O sun! to tell thee how I hate thy beams."

How different was the salutation with which that glorious luminary was welcomed by every soul in our little world ! with what alacrity did we hasten to greet the foremost harbingers of his approach ! But our sentiments, on the first view of the sun, were somewhat different from those of his Tartarian highness :— no great compliment to ourselves, you will say. But let us proceed in due order.

The new year flattered us with a prospect of an improved temperature of the air; but its promise was delusive. The wind fell, and the mercury in the thermometer sunk down to the usual state of this season. On *Sunday*, the 2d *January*, the thermometer indicated the highest temperature to be — 28°, and the barometer 29·6 : on *Monday*, the 3d, the thermometer rose to — 9°, and the barometer fell to 29·4. Notwithstanding the many heavy falls of snow for some time past, the appearance of the land and ice around us was much the same as before. For so intense is the frost, that the particles of snow, more in the form of *spiculæ*, or needles, than of flakes, being perfectly dry, do not adhere together, but are drifted by the wind in all directions, until they lodge in ravines and other hollows, while the heights are, in some places, nearly bare.

In the end of last year and the beginning of this, a number of our people were what is called frost-nipped ; frost-bitten is rather an alarming idea. These accidents generally happened when they were taking brisk exercise in walking or running on shore ; the very time, one should have imagined, when they were the least exposed to them ; and the very means which one should have adopted to prevent such accidents. The cause, however, was at last discovered to be the harshness of the boots worn by the men, which interrupted the circulation of the blood; and when in their place easy boots, made of canvas, and lined with flannel, or other woollen stuff, with soles of raw hide, were used, it is almost incredible how few frost-bites occurred.

In the beginning of January it was first reported to the commander of the expedition, that the sea-scurvy had made its appearance on board the Hecla. The patient first complained of pains in his legs, which were supposed to be rheumatic, but which, when considered in conjunction with the state of his gums, too surely indicated scurvy. This destructive malady rarely makes its first appearance among the officers of a ship ; not so much from any difference in their food (and in this case no difference whatever existed in the provisions of officers and men in either quantity or quality), as from the officers being more attentive than the men to every thing that can affect their health. But the cause of the complaint, in the present instance, lay in this, that the officers' beds were situated in close contact with the ship's sides, and in so far with the external air, whereas the seamen's beds were detached by an open space of a foot and a half.

When the dampness of the patient's bed was suspected to have occasioned his complaint, every bed in the ship was, at stated periods, aired before the fires. The antiscorbutics on board, consisting of various preserved vegetables, or their juices, were immediately employed, and in less than a fortnight the patient was able to take a little exercise between decks. His recovery was also much accelerated by the use of mustard and cresses, a small quantity of which Captain Parry contrived to raise, in shallow boxes filled with mould, placed along the stove-pipe. In this was a confirmation of the fact, that fresh vegetables are the most perfect of all remedies for scorbutic disorders. Having been raised without the influence of day light, the mustard and cresses were colourless, but in all other respects they seemed to possess the qualities belonging to them when raised in the most favourable circumstances.

On the 7th January we had another proof, although certainly no fresh proof was necessary, of the intolerable effect on our feelings produced by cold when accompanied by wind. On that day the mercury in the thermometer fluctuated between $-38°$ and $-40°$: but the wind blew hard from N.N.W. with a heavy drift of snow. So bitterly keen was the sensation of cold, that it was almost impossible to withstand it in moving the short distance from the one ship to the other.

For several days afterwards the aurora borealis frequently appeared, but with very feeble colours; nor were either the magnetic needle or the electric apparatus affected by it.

At noon, on the 11th, the temperature of the external air fell lower than we had ever before experienced it, namely, to $49°$ below zero. But the weather was perfectly calm, so that several officers and men could take exercise on shore without inconveniency.

On such occasions we could not avoid the remark, that several effects of cold, stated to have been experienced by other persons, who had passed the winter in similar climates, were never perceived by us. The excruciating pain in the lungs, the instantaneous conversion of breath-vapour into snow, &c. never came under our observation.

Saturday the 15th was distinguished by the most brilliant, indeed the only very brilliant exhibition of the beauties of the aurora borealis, or northern lights, which we had witnessed since we entered the Arctic regions. The phenomenon first presented a complete arch, nearly in the plane of the meridian. This arch soon broke up, and the common aurora appeared in the southern horizon, such as we had often seen, namely, a pale light seeming to issue from behind a dark cloud; but this darkness might be only the sky itself assuming that colour, from the contrast with the whitish light. The luminous appearance was, with us, confined to the southern horizon, as in Britain it is confined to the northern. We had frequently, in navigating the sounds and straits from Baffin's bay, been induced by the phenomena of the compass, to conceive that we had gone to the northward of the N. magnetic pole of the earth. The appearance of the aurora also to the southward of us may perhaps intimate some kind of relation between the causes of both. This is no new notion; but at any rate no one can be less qualified than I am to advance or to form conjectures on the subject. It has been asserted that a peculiar kind of noise has been heard during remarkable displays of streamers; but although we are placed in a situation the most remote from any terrestrial noises, yet nothing of the kind was ever perceptible by our ears. During the death-like silence in which we are enveloped, we have on many occasions been surprised to notice to what a distance the sound of persons in common conversation on the shore, as well as on board, has been audible. —But as a dry enumeration of circumstances in the order of their chronological succession, especially from my hand, would convey a very imperfect notion of this singularly beautiful phenomenon, I annex a copy of some verses on the subject, which adorn our Arctic Gazette, a production which, wherever imagination and invention are concerned, will not shrink from a comparison with your high born London Gazette. These verses will also serve as a proof that all the snows and ice of N. lat. 75° are not sufficient to quench the flame of British genius.

LINES

Suggested by the brilliant Aurora of 15th January, 1820.

" High quiv'ring in the air, as shadows fly,
The northern lights adorn the azure sky.
Dimm'd by superior blaze the stars retire,
And heav'n's vast concave gleams with sportive fire.
Soft blazing in the east, the orange hue,
The crimson, purple, and ethereal blue,
Form a rich arch, by floating clouds upheld,
High pois'd in air, with awful mystery swelled,
From whose dark centres, with unceasing roll,
Rich coruscations gild the glowing pole.
Their varied hues slow waving o'er the bay,
Eclipse the splendor of the dawning day.
Streamers in quick succession, o'er the sky,
From the arc's centre far diverging fly.
Pencils of rays, pure as the heav'n's own light,
Dart rapid upward to the zenith's height.

> Transfixt with wonder on the frozen flood,
> The blaze of grandeur fired my youthful blood.
> Deep in th' o'erwhelming maze of Nature's laws,
> 'Midst her mysterious gloom I sought the cause:
> But vain the search! inscrutable by man
> Thy works have been, O God! since time began,
> And still shall be.——Then let the thought expire,
> As late the splendors of Aurora's fire
> To dark oblivion sank, in wasting flame,
> Like the dim shadows of departed fame!"

It has been mentioned that our usual serenade consisted in the lugubrious howlings of the ravenous but famished wolves. Like other carnivorous animals they doubtless possess the faculty of devouring prodigious quantities of food when they can obtain it, and of enduring long privation when they cannot. Some of them approached within no great distance of the ships, as we could judge from their howl; but we seldom had a distinct view of them, nor hitherto, in spite of all our contrivances, have we been able to kill or catch one of them. One came over the ice, very close to the ships on the 25th. He was almost entirely white, the body long and lank, as indeed the wolf always seems to be on the continent of Europe, even in his best state. He stood higher on his legs, but much resembled the dogs of the Esquimaux and Greenlanders. His long bushy tail hung down almost to the ground; when running his head was thrown out very low. A dog belonging to the Griper, was for some time in the habit of disappearing from the ship about a certain time of the night, returning on board after some hours' absence. He was more than once seen in company with a wolf, and being mostly of the same colour, may have been well received by that animal. At last he left the ship never more to return; and whether he lost his way, or, which is more probable, that he was destroyed by some stranger wolf, his absence is still unexplained. A large and powerful black dog belonging to the Hecla, used also to frequent the society of his distant relations, the wolves, on shore. One morning he returned home bit and torn about the throat; but about a mile from the ship, following the track in the snow, a considerable quantity of blood and hair was found, showing that the wolf had suffered still more than the dog.

On the 12th of the month experiments were made on the congelation of brandy, on the open deck of the Hecla. The mercury in the thermometer varied from $-42°$ to $-47°$; the barometer from 30·24 to 30·1. A small quantity of strong brandy in 10 minutes began to congeal, and in half an hour it acquired the consistence, and somewhat of the appearance of honey. Remaining exposed on the deck for above an hour, it never became more solid. The experiment was repeated in the evening with the same brandy, and the only change observed was that the congelation became dryer, resembling moist brown sugar. Neither the taste nor the strength of the liquor seemed to be changed, only the frozen part produced a slight smarting on the tongue.

I already told you of the loss we sustained by the bursting of bottles containing our lemon juice. Similar accidents continuing to happen, it became necessary to reduce the quantity served out every day to the ships' companies to three quarters of the usual allowance, that is to three quarters of an ounce, which, when mixed with sugar, every man was obliged to swallow every morning in the presence of an officer.

When a highly valued friend is expected to return to us after a long absence, is it not natural not only to make all due preparation for his reception, but also to be looking out for his appearance days perhaps before, as we well know, he can possibly arrive? you will not then be surprised that we should be anxiously anticipating the return of the sun, to put an end to our tedious months of idleness and apprehension. On *Tuesday* the 25th *January*, each man in the Hecla (for her main-top mast being preserved in its place, she could command the highest point of view) without distinction went up to the mast-head, or the crow's nest, to look out for the sun. To prevent injury from the weather in that exposed situation, each person was to stay aloft only ten minutes at a time. This was regularly done for nine days together; for so long was it before the sun was visible, above the horizon, from the deck. This was not done from any doubt of the day, on which he was to appear; for that is a matter of previous calculation, founded on the latitude of the place of observation and the sun's place in the ecliptic. Introduce the lower half or other part of a straight walking-stick into a canal or a vessel of water, in an inclined position, and it will seem to be broken or bent upwards at the surface of the water. That is, you see the immersed portion of the stick higher than it actually is. This effect is produced in transparent fluids of all kinds. As far as regards this effect, the atmosphere which envelopes our globe is a fluid. When, therefore, the sun or any other heavenly body comes near to our horizon, the rays of light proceeding from him being bent, cause him to be visible to us some time before he be actually come to the right line joining his body and our eye be truly a tangent to the surface of the sphere. This inflection of the rays of light is termed refraction, and it varies according to certain properties of the atmosphere at the time of observation. When we look at a distant object along the surface of the globe, the visual rays pass through the greatest body of atmosphere; the refraction is of course the greatest, and in proportion as the object rises above the horizon, the refraction diminishes until the object become vertical to the observer, and there refraction ceases. To atmospheric refraction we owe the fact that the sun, moon, &c. must be seen some time before the body be actually and geometrically above our horizon; and must also continue to be seen some time after it is actually below the horizon. Now it was an object of great importance to us, who in our courses must be guided by the apparent, rather than by the real position of objects, to ascertain, by observation, the quantity of refractive power possessed by the atmosphere around us. For this purpose, therefore, our observations on the appearance of the sun were instituted a number of days before that on which, by calculation, he was actually to be above our horizon.

Towards the end of the month a halo, or ring of a pale light, appeared round the moon, of about $22°\frac{1}{4}$ radius; and it was observed. that such appearances usually began at the full moon. On the 28th, although the atmosphere was particularly clear and serene, with a beautiful red colour spread over the southern horizon, yet no sun was perceived from the mast-head. As a proof, however, of the strength of light proceeding from the sun, although invisible, and reflected from our atmosphere, I must mention that, at noon of the same day, no fixed star, of even the first magnitude, was perceptible by the naked eye: but Mars was plainly seen. In the end of the month some of the ship's ports were opened to admit the light for carrying on, or at least for commencing, some works below, and so appearing, in some shape, to prepare for continuing our voyage.

At last, to our great joy, *Thursday*, the 3d of *February*, about twenty minutes before noon, came down from the main-top of the Hecla, and quickly spread among the crews, the ravishing news that the glorious, beneficent source of light and heat to our globe, and to the whole solar system of globes, was actually visible, over the land which shut in our harbour on the south. Thus may be said to have terminated our dreary period of night, after a duration of eighty-four days from the 11th November. The 4th of November, as was observed in a former letter, was properly the last day on which, in our position, the sun could be seen above our horizon from the surface of the sea, according to calculation of his place. But such was the effect of refraction that, at noon of the 11th of that month, about one half of the sun's body was perceived from the main-top of the Hecla, fifty feet above the water, that is, the ice in which she lay. Thus his absence was shortened twelve days from the ninety-six indicated by calculation, a favour conferred on us by the refraction of the atmosphere, aided by the elevation of the eye above the sea. From the upper part of the sun ascended, for about 3° of eleva-

PREPARING STONES FOR BALLAST.

tion, a column of pale red light, varying in its brightness very quickly, and visible for above half an hour before and after noon. At the same time, a little to the eastward of the sun, was perceived an appearance greatly resembling distant land. This appearance had been observed several times before, since we lay in Winter Harbour, but never so distinctly. It seemed to end in an abrupt, well-defined manner, in a S. by E. direction.

On *Friday* the 4th, the sun was again seen from the main-top; but it was not until noon of *Monday* the 7th that he first appeared clear and distinct, and a very faint mock-sun, or parhelion, was perceived on his eastern side, at about the distance of 22°, the general angular distance of all such phenomena as we had observed. It is, perhaps, remarkable, that this distance always exceeds, or comes short, by a small quantity, of the angle formed by the planes of the ecliptic and equator, from which arises the admirable variation of length of days and nights all over the globe. Yet as the parhelion is supposed to be caused wholly by atmospherical refraction and reflection, no connexion between their powers and the obliquity of the ecliptic can easily be traced: but, as Pope says,

"Even Crane Court knows not yet all Nature's laws.

You are not aware, perhaps, that Crane Court, in Fleet Street, was formerly the seat of the Royal Society now assembled in Somerset Place, and that the same place, as I understood in London, has lately become the residence of another society, also devoted to the study of philosophical subjects.

Although the sun was visible for a very short space only at noon, yet his daily path descended so little below our horizon, that, from eight in the morning to four in the afternoon, we had light enough to perform several kinds of work on the outside of the ships. It was not, therefore, longer necessary to invent labour of different kinds to maintain the men in health by employment of various sorts. The first necessary occupation was to collect and bring down to the beach stone for ballast to the ships, especially to the Hecla, which carried various stores for the Griper, as well as for herself, and by the consumption of these and provisions was now considerably lightened. The coldest part of the season was now, however, supposed to be approaching; it therefore became of the highest importance to expose the men as little as possible to the severity of the climate; for even the slightest hurt it was extremely difficult to cure.

You cannot well conceive the satisfaction felt on board ship on *Friday* the 11th, when the sun, although rising but one degree above the horizon, was able, in some measure, to influence the thermometer, which rose from $-40°$ to $-35°$, when directly exposed to his heat. That this effect was produced by the sun's immediate action was clear from this, that as he declined and disappeared, the instrument returned to the former temperature of 40o.

In speaking of the aurora borealis, during which a noise proceeding from it has been reported to be heard, I mentioned that no such noise could ever be heard by us, although in a situation perfectly devoid of all noise of any other kind. We have of late, however, since increased light allows people to walk to some distance from the ships, been amazed to hear them conversing in an ordinary tone of voice, during the severe cold, at the distance of a mile. A man was heard singing to himself on the beach on the 11th still farther off. Some officers walking on the beach to leeward of the ships, at least two miles off, perceived a strong smell of smoke on the surface of the ground. This could proceed from the ships only, and showed that the very low temperature of the atmosphere prevented the smoke from ascending. What was taken for land in the southward was again perceived this day, and in the same abrupt form as before. That land does really exist in that quarter may, therefore, be very probable.

It is scarcely necessary to observe, that the temperature on board was necessarily higher than that on shore, the difference varying from 2° to 5°. On *Monday* the 14th, the thermometer on board was at 48°, but that at the house, constructed on shore for the instruments, clocks, &c. fell to 52° at six in the morning. The barometer stood at 29·53 inches. At noon the thermometer in the shade rose one degree; but within two hours it returned to 52_o. Notwithstanding this intense cold, yet as the wind was light from the westward, and the weather remarkably fine, we took exercise on shore without any inconveniency, just in our usual winter's dress.

In one of the works of the celebrated electrician, Dr. Franklin, I remember to have read of experiments he made on the different degrees of heat, imbibed by substances of the same quality, but of different colours, when exposed to the direct rays of the sun. Small pieces of woollen cloth from a tailor's pattern-book were laid out on the snow in a bright sun-shiny morning. They were of various colours, black, deep blue, light blue, green, purple, red, yellow, white, &c. In a few hours the black pattern having absorbed the sun's heat, was warmed, melted the snow under it, and sunk so low in it as to be below the stroke of his rays. The dark blue sunk almost as deep as the black. The other colours were deep in the snow in proportion to the deepness of their hue: and the white cloth remained on the surface of the snow, not entering it at all, because it repelled the rays and acquired no sensible warmth. " What signifies philosophy that does not apply to some use ?" This was the Doctor's standing question : he accordingly points out a number of uses to which his experiments might be applied. A result in confirmation of the above occurred to ourselves. A board against which the thermometers were hung was painted black on one side, but on the other was white, or of the natural colour of the wood. The thermometer on the black side never fell below—52°, but that on the white side sunk to—54°. The board was erected on the ice, perhaps one hundred yards from either of the ships: no effect could therefore be produced on the thermometers by any local heat on board.

The most intense cold hitherto indicated by the spirit thermometer occurred on Tuesday the 15th. From 4, P. M. of the preceding afternoon, to 7, A. M. of this day, the thermometer fixed on the ice, between the ships and the shore, never rose above—54° and at 6 in the morning, she fell to—55° The weather was all the time clear and nearly calm : but a light breeze springing up from the northward, the temperature rose to —49°. Observing this extraordinary depression of the thermometer, an officer of the Hecla carried up to the main-top a quart bottle filled with fresh water, or water procured by melting snow. There pouring the water through a small cullender, the drops were found to have congealed into irregular spheres before they reached the roof of the housing constructed over the ship, a distance of about 40 feet.

On the same day experiments were made on the congelation of mercury. When congealed by the cold of the atmosphere, which, when the mercury is pure, happens at 40° below zero, or 72° below the freezing point of water, the solid mass was beat on an anvil reduced to the same temperature ; but in this state, the mercury was not very malleable ; for it always broke after a few strokes of the hammer.

At this time, from the cheering presence of the sun for some hours above the horizon, the length of day-light, and the irresistible desire to admit light into the cabin of the Hecla, the Commander directed the dead-lights, or strong shutters, which block up the stern windows on the outside, to be opened. The glass frames within were double about two feet asunder, and between them were curtains of baize nailed to the frames. On removing the dead-lights, the interval was absolutely filled with ice, from the vapour of the cabin, and the cold entered so powerfully through the glass, that up to this day the cold is there much less tolerable than upon deck. A thermometer on the floor of the cabin, even when the officers were in it, stood at 19° above zero, and one suspended in the upper part of the cabin, never rose above 34° or a little above the freezing point of water.

Hitherto all our attention and efforts had been occupied in providing against cold : now we were exposed to great loss from the opposite—fire. About 10 A. M. of Thursday the 24th past, flames were seen to break out from the building erected on the beach, on our arrival in Winter Harbour, to contain the astronomical clocks, transit-instrument, &c. At this moment the men were taking their usual run round the ships' decks, and had on warm clothing. When the fire was discovered, men and officers hastened on shore to the house, which was framed of double fir plank, with a stuffing of moss between them. Pulling off the roof with ropes, and knocking down part of the sides, snow was thrown in in such quantities as to extinguish the flames before they reached that end where the clocks, &c. were standing in their cases. These were removed, and the ruined part of the building was covered with snow ; and all the most valuable instruments being preserved, the search for other articles was put off, until more moderate weather should allow the men to dig among the ruins, without certain injury to their health. While all were employed in quenching the fire, our medical gentlemen were in constant rounds, with several assistants, rubbing with snow the white spots on the faces of those who were busy at the work, to counteract the frost-bites continually making their appearance. Notwithstanding every precaution, however, above twelve ases of frosting were added to the sick in both ships. The most severe sufferer of all was the artillery-soldier of the Hecla, who, with the serjeant, was in the house where the fire began. Anxious to save the dipping needle belonging to that ship, they ran out with it; but the soldier not having time to put on his mittens, in a short time had his fingers so benumbed, that the animation was completely suspended. When taken on board and his hands immersed in a vessel of water, for the purpose of gradually thawing them, so intense was the cold in his hands, that the surface of the water was immediately covered with a thin coat of ice. You may also judge of the degree of cold in the air, from what I have just said, that great as was the heat from the fire, it was not sufficient to prevent a number of those employed in saving the instruments and extinguishing the flames from frost-bites. The misfortune was occasioned as I understand, by some clothes drying near the stove, which took fire, and communicated it to the dry matting which lined the sides of the house.

The return of the sun has lighted up in us all new prospects, new hopes, and imaginations : but on these topics more correct notions will be contained in my next. In the mean time I must bid you adieu.

Your's, &c. &c.

LETTER XI.

DEAR THOMAS,
                    Winter Harbour, May 1st, 1820.
IN my last letter of the 1st March, I mentioned the hazard to which the expedition was exposed, by the conflagration of the instrument-house, erected on the shore. Had the astronomical clocks, the transit-instrument, the dipping-needle, or the dipping-sector been destroyed, or materially injured, several important purposes of our adventure must have been frustrated, several of its chief objects must have been unattainable. Without them we should not have been able to ascertain the position we occupied on the face of the globe with that accuracy required for the purposes of science. With instruments of ordinary correctness of construction, the latitude of a place may be discovered with sufficient precision. For such a purpose a well-constructed Hadley's quadrant or sextant, answers very well. As you have frequently seen and examined that admirable instrument, I need say no more about it than, that by the combination of the principles of optics and geometry, the altitudes of the celestial bodies, and their relative positions, and angular or apparent distances, may be determined on ship-board, notwithstanding the incessant motion of the vessel, with equal ease as upon solid ground. When, however, you have fixed a position in regard to its northing or southing, that is, its perpendicular distance N. or S. from the equinoctial line, or in a contrary direction from the terrestrial poles, you have obtained but one of the elements necessary for fixing its position on the globe. For all places situated on the parallel which encircles the earth at that distance from the line, will have the same latitude. To determine with strict precision the situation of any particular spot, you must also know its easting or westing, that is, its perpendicular distance E. or W. from some determined point on its own parallel; that is, you must fix its longitude. Longitude and latitude are strange terms to be employed in relation to a globe or sphere, for it is essential to that body that, in whatever direction you measure its circumference, the dimensions must be absolutely equal among themselves. But these terms have been conveyed down to us from very remote times: they have long been correctly understood; and now to introduce others strictly expressive of their value, would only savour of affectation, and produce extreme confusion. That our earth was a ball, globe, or sphere, was known to the philosophers of antiquity. They did not, however, conceive more than the

more temperate portions of the earth to be habitable. The burning south, and the frozen north, were alike imagined to be unfit for the habitation of human beings. The Greeks, from whom we have our earliest notions of geography and astronomy, were acquainted with little else of the earth than the countries bordering on the Mediterranean, and certain portions of southern Asia; their knowledge consequently extended much more from east to west than from north to south. The former dimensions they naturally considered as the length, or longitude of the world, and the latter as its breadth, or latitude.

The latitude of any place is always equal to the elevation of the nearest pole above the true horizon of that place. An observer placed on the equinoctial has both poles in the horizon : neither of them has any altitude, or elevation, nor has he any latitude. An observer at the north pole will have the celestial pole (the pole-star for example) vertical, or $90°$ above the horizon all around; his latitude is consequently $90°$ N. But the north polestar is not always visible, nor is it so easy to ascertain the elevation of that star above the horizon in the night time: in such cases we must resort to the sun, whose place in the ecliptic every day and hour is known : by this and his meridian, or other altitude, the latitude of the observer may be calculated with the greatest accuracy. Thus latitudes may be ascertained by a process extremely simple, when compared with that necessary for discovering the longitude. To determine the easting or westing of a ship or a place, with respect to some established first meridian, methods have been devised of great accuracy: but here the difficulty occurs, that of those methods some of great correctness, when practised on land, are next to impracticable on sea. Speaking in common language, as I have all along done in these observations, the earth has a rotation on its axis from west to east, once in a day of 24 hours; or of 15 degrees of longitude in every hour of time. Hence, if a certain phenomenon, the commencement of an eclipse of the sun for instance, be calculated to happen at a certain hour, as noon in London, that phenomenon will not begin at a place situated $75°$ W. from the meridian of London, until 5 hours later, or at 5 in the afternoon. On the other hand, an observer situated $75°$ E. from the meridian of London, will observe the commencement of the eclipse 5 hours sooner, or at 7 in the morning. Hence, by observing the precise time of any celestial appearance, and comparing it with the time fixed for its appearance at a given first meridian, we can discover how much we are removed in longitude,(not in distance,) E. or W. from the meridian. Now all this is most easy in theory or on paper, but it is most difficult in practice. This earth is not a perfect sphere; the atmosphere changes the appearances and places of objects, without our being able precisely to value the changes produced; there is always some uncertainty in fixing the point where the phenomenon in question actually does take place; nor is it possible to determine with absolute precision the instant of time of its appearance.

Were it possible to construct a machine which should maintain, for the duration of a voyage across the wide seas, an absolute rate of motion, or even with an equal rate of error, the time elapsed between any celestial occurrence in the place of observation, and that of the first meridian, would at once point out the longitude of the observer. To attain this perfection in mechanism has long occupied the attention of many eminent artists, and men of science; and the progress towards this perfection has already been very great. Clocks moved by weights, and regulated by pendulums, are not fit for use at sea, where the vessel is in continual, and sometimes in violent irregular motion. To these objections watches actuated by springs are much less liable. Watches for sea-use have been known by various names; marine-watches, time-pieces, time-keepers, time-measurers or chronometers; the last now generally employed. Neither you nor I, my dear Thomas, are sufficiently acquainted with the principles of mechanics, of natural philosophy, and natural history, to comprehend the construction of a chronometer. Of this, however, I can assure you, that the more you consider their conformation, and the multiplied contrivances for obviating or balancing the alterations to which every machine must of necessity be liable, it is far more a subject of admiration, that chronometers should persevere for any length of time in equable motion, than that they should not yet have arrived nearer to perfection.

In connexion with the chronometer is the instrument for ascertaining the transit or passage of any celestial body over the meridian of the place of observation. By the instruments for measuring the dip, as it is called, of the surface of the ocean, (or of ice) we learn to ascertain the real elevation of any body above the horizon. By them, also, we discover the convexity of the earth, which, as you have heard and read, is by no means a perfect sphere, nor probably a regular figure of revolution of any kind. By the dip we seamen mean the depression of the surface of the waters below a tangent to the earth, drawn from the place of observation. The ascertainment of the dip tends likewise to determine the actual figure of the earth. But a material obstacle to the accuracy of observations of the positions of celestial bodies, with relation to the earth, arises from the refractive power of the atmosphere, a power of which we have no means to know the effect, but by experiment: for here theory is of very little service.
——— But on this topic. I have already given you a few cursory

remarks————Let us now return to our ordinary statement of occurrences.

————My last letter reached down to the 1st *March*; I have now of course the affairs of two months to communicate to you.

March was ushered in by very encouraging omens. The horizon in the S.E. for half an hour before the sun rose on Wednesday, the 1st of the month, displayed a bright red light which seemed to announce his appearance half an hour before his time. The weather being moderate and clear, people were employed in removing whatever had been covered by the ruins of the instrument-house on shore, and preparations were begun for the erection of a new one. Some officers in their walk on shore observed the snow, where most exposed to the sun, to be glazed and slippery; a symptom of thaw, as far as his immediate power was concerned. It is impossible for you to conceive, and I am sure I will not attempt to describe, the delight felt on this information. We were comparing it with what we had seen in more favoured climates, and some of us, I for one, began after making all reasonable allowances for latitude, &c. to calculate the day when we might hope to be released from our miserable imprisonment. But this was truly *compter sans son hôte*. Little did I know the landlord who had so hospitably retained us for so many months: his kindness was not to be so easily satisfied. Some changes, nevertheless, were perceptible in the state of the weather. In the night of the 2d *March* the wind blew strong from the southward, a quarter from which a gale was very seldom experienced. In the morning at 9, a parhelion appeared on each side of the sun, about the usual distance of 22°. Disappearing soon afterwards, they re-appeared at 2 P. M., and, at the same time, came on a thick fog or haze. This was considered as a favourable symptom, as indicating a moister and softer temperature in the atmosphere. On the 5th a light breeze coming from the southward, the thermometer rose from — 26° early in the morning to — 15° at noon, and the weather, on the whole, became to our feelings so mild and pleasant that, after divine service, as many of the officers and men as could be spared, and were able, took a long walk on the heights round the harbour. This was the first day which we could regard as in some sort resembling spring, that is, the spring of lat. 75°.

On *Monday* the 6th, at 8 A. M. the mercury in the thermometer rose to zero, the beginning of the positive scale: a height to which it had before attained only on the 17th December and the 5th of November preceding. The wind went round from S.E. to S., and then W. to N; the night a succession of heavy squalls and calms, a kind of weather never before observed. On the 7th some snow that had lodged on the black-painted part of the stern of the Hecla, which was immediately exposed to the sun, was observed to be melted; while snow on the yellow parts remained unaffected by the warmth. This incident you will think a matter of no great moment; but to us it appeared in a very different light. It proved that the influence of the sun was increasing; and it confirmed what was already noticed respecting the Franklinian experiments on the power of coloured substances in repelling or retaining heat. The black paint retained, and the light yellow repelled it. The thermometer exposed to the sun, under the stern of the Hecla, gave a temperature as high as 35° above zero, or 3° above the freezing point of water. About a mile in a direction N.E. from the bottom of the harbour is an eminence, thence called North-east Hill, about two hundred and fifty feet above the level of the sea, the highest land in our neighbourhood. From this point the view extends to a considerable distance to S. and S.E , and from it, six or seven miles from the land, were perceived a range of hummocks (a sea term for low detached hillocks on land, and thence applied to ice,) thrown up to a considerable height, by the pressure of the outer ice upon that which was joined to the shore. While the weather continued in its mild and moderate state, the opportunity was taken to re-build the house for the instruments that had been burnt down. This was the work of a few days only, when the astronomical clocks were re-placed. Before the conflagration, the observations made principally related to the distance of the moon from certain stars, and the elevation of these last above the horizon, in order to ascertain the apparent time. Now it was intended to institute a series of observations on the distance of certain stars from the zenith, for the purpose of discovering the refraction of the atmosphere, by comparing their apparent with their real distances. This last operation, however, it was found could not be performed; for the repeating circle, the only instrument sent out, adapted to the purpose, ceased to be of use in temperatures below zero. By the intensity of the cold, the joints and other moveable parts of the instrument were fixed, and the spirit in the level was contracted, so as to be of no use. The two metals, also, of which the instrument was composed, brass and steel, being unequally affected by the cold, it became quite unmanageable. Respecting the important experiments on the pendulum, for ascertaining the proportion between its length and the number of vibrations in a given time, in the view of determining the deviation of the form of the earth from a perfect sphere, it was deemed proper to defer them until the season should be farther advanced, and the weather become so mild as to allow the instruments to be handled without injury to the observers.

The first week of March was remarkable for the frequent appearance of the parhelion, or mock-sun, particularly on the 4th and the 8th. This last came on about 1 P. M. when the sun had not sunk much below the meridian, his altitude being about 20°. At the usual distance of 22° or 23° from the sun was a halo, the lowest portion of which was, consequently, below our horizon. Across the sun's body, parallel to the horizon, ran a circle of pale white light quite round the heavens; and on each side, where this bar crossed the halo, appeared a parhelion, so bright as to make it painful to the eye to examine them for some time. So perfect were these mock suns, that had the real sun been concealed, either of them might have been taken for it behind a cloud. An hour or more after this phenomenon was observed, higher up towards the zenith appeared a small portion, or the lower segment of another halo, but very faint in its colour. During the 9th we had a very hard gale from N.W., with a severe snow-drift, which appeared to rise up from the high grounds a mile or two off, just like the dust carried up in a pillar by a whirlwind, or like the representation of a water-spout at sea. A few days after this, two men of both ships were rated on the sick-list for the scurvy, but none of them very ill.

Thursday 16*th* was closed our arctic theatre, by an address adapted to the occasion, from the gentleman whose pen and voice were employed for its opening. The season was now so far advanced, and the day was now so long, for the equinox was at hand, that the men were no longer in want of healthful occupation, nor were the officers compelled to invent employment and exercise for them and for themselves. The approach of the equinox brought to us, as no doubt it did to you, storms of wind with great variations of temperature, which were as severely felt as in the depth of winter. Whatever, therefore, may be the cause of this tempestuous weather, at the moment when both sun and moon are in the planes of both ecliptic and equator, when the day and the night are of equal duration all over the globe, the action of that cause seems to extend to all parts of our globe. The weather had been so boisterous for some time prior to the equinox of September, that we could not discover whether it ought or not to be considered as connected with the equinox.

I already mentioned that one of the men who were in the instrument house when it took fire had his hands completely benumbed by the cold. When he was taken on board the Hecla his hands were as hard as marble, and were so extremely cold that the water into which they were dipped was quickly covered with a coat of ice. Every method was employed to restore the animation and sensibility of the parts, but all in vain; so that it became necessary to take off the extremities of the fingers of both hands. It was remarked by our medical gentlemen, that the effects produced in destroying life in the parts by the cold were quite different from those arising from what they call sphacelus, or gangrene, or in common language mortification. The mortified parts underwent no change in form or in size ; but some days before the operation the nails and skin of the fingers fell off. In treating frost-bites the first thing done was to rub the affected parts well with snow, and then to immerse them in cold water to raise their temperature and restore feeling. When these applications did not succeed in a short time, exciting plasters or cataplasms were in most cases applied with success.

On *Monday* the 20th *March* some seamen reported that, while they were on shore procuring stone for ballast, they saw one of those sea-gulls formerly mentioned, called by the Dutch Greenlanders the burgomaster. It certainly appears strange that this bird, which draws its food from the sea, could subsist in this quarter in winter, where doubtless no water free from ice was to be found : but to see even this single bird was a pleasing occurrence, for even the wolves and foxes had now for some time forsaken us.

It was not a little distressing for us in this ship, that the number of persons on our sick-list should, in the latter end of March, be more than double that of the Hecla; and of those in the Griper four were scorbutic cases. The cause of this disproportion was, undoubtedly, the extreme moisture or damp, in the sleeping-places of the Griper, where the whole ship's company, amounting to thirty-six persons, were confined within comparatively narrow space, relatively to the fifty-eight on board the Hecla, a vessel of twice her capacity. To remedy this defect, it was recommended to remove the fixed bed-places which obstructed the circulation of fresh air, and of warmth from the fires : hammocks were, in consequence, substituted for the beds. Our commander, Lieutenant Liddon, whose health had been for some time in an alarming state, was removed from his fixed bed to a cot at some distance from the ship's side. From that day he happily recovered so fast that, in a few weeks, he was able to take exercise every fine day without inconvenience, although the mercury stood greatly below zero. In digging a hole through the ice a little way off from the ships, where the depth of water was known to exceed four fathoms, the thickness of the ice was found to be between six and seven feet, besides the snow on the surface about nine inches deep. All this quantity had been formed since the beginning of the preceding September. Whether the increase in future will much exceed the quantity thawed on the surface by the sun in clear weather, time alone can show. To give you, however, some notion of the difference of temperature in the sun at and after noon, and in the shade, I may mention that, by observation of two thermometers, the one in the sun at noon of *Saturday* the 25th *March,* stood at 30 degrees above zero, while that in the shade was at 25 degrees below zero. At 1 P. M. sun + 17°, shade — 22°. At 2 P. M. sun + 25°, shade — 22°. At 3 P. M. sun + 21°, shade — 22° On *Sunday* the 26th, the twilight was very sensible in the northern part of the heavens at midnight ; and we could scarcely persuade ourselves that so little time had passed over us since we were involved in constant darkness. On the following day a fox was found dead in one of the traps, in all respects resembling the one formerly caught.

On the 28th an officer of the Hecla, who had taken a walk on the heights to the westward of the ships, perceived the appearance of land to the southward, formerly mentioned, still terminating abruptly in a direction a little to the eastward of south from our position. The repeated recurrence of this appearance really seems to prove land to exist in that quarter, and that it is not the effect of any atmospherical illusion.

If the 1st of April be renowned for deception in your part of the world, it has had just the contrary effect in ours. A few weeks ago a party on shore having gone about three miles northward from the ships found a flat stone having the letter P cut on it. This letter being evidently the work of some hand, no small surprise was excited by its discovery, as it intimated that we were not the first visitors of the country. This day the stone was brought on board, and on enquiry among the men of both crews it was discovered that Peter Fisher, one of the party lost with Mr. Fyfe the Greenland master of our ship, in September last, had in his wanderings begun to cut his name on a stone on which he rested himself. The curious part of the business is this, that instead of penetrating to a great distance northwards into the interior of the country, they had wandered upwards of twenty miles eastwardly from the place where they went ashore. That the man should employ himself in such a work in his situation at that time is a true picture of a seaman. When he came on board this ship he amazed us by his fresh appearance and the little concern he felt for the dangers from which he just escaped. As to the manner in which he and his companions had lived while they were lost, " As for that (said he) the prince himself never lived better; for we had game for breakfast, game for dinner, and game for supper."

Early one morning in the beginning of April, we witnessed an effect of refraction not uncommon in seas where ice is abundant. Immediately in contact with the summits of the hummocks or eminences of ice, appeared the representation of them correct but reversed. And on the 8th, the weather being clear and calm, the apparent land of the same description was once more observed beyond the ice to the southward.

Halos and mock-suns were now no strangers, but on *Sunday* the 9th *April*, a combination of them appeared very different from any thing we had ever seen before. It lasted, in a general sense, from a little after noon till 6 P. M.; but the most striking appearance for variety of colours was about 1 P. M. The sun was then elevated about 23° above the southern horizon, just enough to show the usual halo complete above the ground. Parallel to the horizon was the plane of a circle of white light through the sun, which completely surrounded the heavens, and at its intersection with the perpendicular halo were, as formerly, two parhelia, exhibiting the colours of the rainbow. Immediately under the sun, at the point where the halo grazed the horizon, instead of the column of light seemingly supporting the sun, as observed on the 8th March, was a parhelion of a dazzling brightness. Above the sun, a little way from the halo, was an arch of an elliptic rather than a circular form as it appeared to us, who were perhaps below its plane, which probably passed through the sun, with an inclination to the horizontal circle beforementioned equal to the angle formed by the ecliptic and equator. Beyond this elliptic arch was a circle partly prismatic, at the distance of 45°, or double that of the first perpendicular circle from the sun. This outer circle was not, however, complete to us, the lower portion passing under our horizon. At the points where it touched the horizon, and at its superior part, were small portions of circles turning away from it. It was observed that when these circles and mock-suns appear, although the weather could not be called snowy or even hazy, yet the air seemed to be filled with a multitude of small particles of snow, strongly reflecting the sun's rays.

At midnight preceding this remarkable phenomenon, the light was strong enough to enable an observer to read off the degrees of the thermometer.

The day and the light were now long, but the temperature continued still to fall very low. The sun was now above the horizon for 17 hours, yet the thermometer frequently sunk to 31° below zero, a fact which occasioned very uneasy feelings respecting the term of our release from bondage. But a sky without a cloud was not fitted to reflect the sun's rays, and an extent of land and sea uniformly white with ice and snow was not fitted to retain them. Nor was it until vapours began to collect in the atmosphere, and parts of the land to be uncovered, that any certain signs of thaw could be perceived.

On the 14th a dog belonging to us returned from the land, after an absence of several days, without any visible injury. The day before he was seen in the company of a wolf, when another dog making up to the stranger was very roughly received and returned in great haste howling. The wolf appeared about the size of a Newfoundland dog, but the tail was different, being so long as to reach down to the ground.

On the 20th the wind blew from the south-east quarter with a constant fall of snow, of which the *spicula*, or pointed particles, although larger than at any time since the former summer, could scarcely be called flakes. The weather soon after became milder, and on the 25th, at 8 A. M. the mercury rose to 10° above zero. On the two following days observations were made on the difference of emperature in the sun and in the shade, by suspending two perfectly equal thermometers on a line stretched between two posts fixed in the snow near the observatory; the one being exposed to the direct rays of the sun, and the other in the shade of the building. At half past one P. M. of the 26th April, the thermometer in the sun stood at 17°, and that in the shade at 6° 5', both above zero. At 2 o'clock, sun + 22°, shade + 7°. At 3 hours 18 minutes, sun + 24° 5', shade 7° 6'. At 11 hours 40 minutes of the 27th, sun + 24°, shade + 9°. At noon, sun + 21°, shade + 7°. Both days the weather almost calm. On the morning of the 27th the bedding of the ships was hung up to air among the rigging, for the first time for eight months preceding. While this was doing the births and bed-places were well fumigated with a mixture of gunpowder and vinegar, as had been practised once every week during winter. By the change in the nature of the snow from a fine dusty loose appearance, the continual sport of the winds, to flakes in some degree adhering together, the country round the harbour appears more generally covered with snow than formerly; for it is not now so liable to be blown off from the upper exposed surfaces and drifted into the hollows. The snow that lay on the roofing over the ships' decks is nearly all gone. Patches of black turf begin to peep through the snow where exposed to the sun, and the few plants which the soil affords are in progress to budding at the edges of the melted snow. For a month past the south-east winds have shown themselves warmer than those from any other quarter. On *Sunday* the 30th the change of temperature was so considerable that the thermometer stood at 32° above zero, which with you is the freezing point of water; but with us might with more propriety be termed the thawing point of snow and ice. Such an occurrence we have not witnessed since the 9th September last. So sensible besides was this alteration to the feelings of the men. that it required positive orders from the commander to prevent them from making changes in their dress, an experiment which must have exposed them to serious inconveniences. To make you understand the nature of these changes of the weather, you must be told that in the course of the last twenty days of April the thermometer ranged no less than 64 degrees, that is to say, on the 10th the mercury was at 32° below zero; on the 22d it had risen to zero; and on the 30th to 32° above zero, the point of freezing and thawing water. In the view of this rapid alteration of temperature, even the least sanguine in the expedition looked forward to the end of June as the period of our release from our present confinement in Winter Harbour.

The large wolf, already mentioned, has for some days kept within sight of the ships, and been visited by the same dog. The wolf is, however, too powerful for our traps, and so wary that we have never got near enough to try a shot.

As our attention and thoughts are now turned to the necessary preparations for availing ourselves of the favourable weather for our departure from this station, of which you may imagine us to be now heartily tired, I must close this epistle with best and kindest wishes for you all.

Ever your's, &c. &c.

LETTER XII.

DEAR BROTHER, *Winter Harbour, 1st July*, 1820.

THE material improvement in the weather in the end of April led to the commencement of the proposed observations, relative to the determining the length of a pendulum, to vibrate seconds of time in the latitude of Winter Harbour. The astronomical clocks were accordingly carried ashore from the Hecla, and the observations were began. May, however, came in with a very different aspect; for on *Monday* the first of that month, the day in which I closed my last letter, the wind and snow-drift came away so keenly from the northward that the requisite degree of warmth it was impossible to keep up in the observatory. The door being completely blocked by the drift, it was necessary to communicate with the astronomer, Captain Sabine, and his attendants, otherwise than by a small window. At midnight the sun was visible on the northern meridian for the first time this year. In a few days the high grounds were again uncovered, the gales having drifted off the snow, now again dry and loose. On the 3d and 4th days of the month the thermometer fell to —26°.

On this latter day the men began to clear away the snow which had been necessarily heaped up against the ships' sides, with the view of preventing the escape of the internal warmth, as must have been the case had they been constantly in contact with the intense cold of the external air. Snow you have read is a bad conductor of heat. The accumulated snow also prevented the ice from forming to a greater thickness than it would otherwise have done.

Thursday 4*th* appeared an order, to take effect on the 10th, reducing the daily allowance of provisions, of all sorts, to two-thirds of the usual quantity. The ships were victualled for only two years, and one was now expired since we left the Thames; the necessity of this reduction was so apparent to all on board both ships, that not a man showed the least reluctance, officers or men, to comply with the regulation. It was also ordered, that whatever game should be brought on board should be used as common property, not in addition to the regulated allowance, but in its place as far as it should go. These game-laws, as we called them, were applied without the smallest distinction of commander, officer, or man, of both ships. The only exception was in favour of the sick, to whom fresh meat was furnished whenever it could be procured. The first opportunity of affording this relief, after being deprived of fresh provisions of any kind for six months together, was on the 13th, when a ptarmigan, or grouse, was shot by Mr. Beverley, our surgeon. This was, perhaps, the bird that was seen the day before. But in a few days several more were seen, and their tracks on the snow were so numerous, as to show that many birds were now arrived in the island. When I say arrived, I conclude that these grouse came from some more favoured region; for had they remained in our quarter of the world, some of them must have been observed. It was remarkable, also, that they were first seen in the first good weather after the beginning of constant sunshine, which took place on the 1st. I have understood here, that in the winter time grouse are found in vast numbers in the neighbourhood of Hudson's Bay; a fact which would probably be confirmed were we at all acquainted with that part of North America which lies farther to the westward, and the nearest continent to the southward of our station. An officer of the Hecla saw four ptarmigans on the wing on the 15th, which seemed to have crossed the sea, or rather the ice, from the southward. Grouse are not the only birds already seen around us: snow-buntings and a raven have been observed. The latter was prevented, by the approach of a party on shore, from falling a prey to a wolf, who, instead of alarming the bird, by a direct attack, moved round him, closing in gradually, until the raven was disturbed by our people and flew off.

Wednesday, 17*th May,* several persons out on shooting expeditions have been affected with what is called snow-blindness, a very painful disorder, beginning with a feeling as if sand or dust was in the eyes. The Indians of North America, I am told, cure this complaint by holding the eyes over the steam of warm water, to take off the irritation : but our medical gentlemen think a much more efficacious method will be, to bathe the eyes with a weak solution of sugar of lead, and cover them from the light. A piece of black crape to hang before the face as a veil, will also be of great service. This I remember to have read was practised by different persons in their expeditions to Mont Blanc, and other elevated snowy parts of the Alps. At this time light vapours were perceived rising from the ground, which produced a tremulous motion in the atmosphere, and in the night cooled into the form of thick fog.

This same day the people finished the cutting of the ice round the ships, which was found to be about six feet in thickness, or a foot and a half more than the general thickness a little way off. The operation exposed the people to wet and cold, but it was cheerfully performed as a leading step to extricate the ships from their long imprisonment. The ships having been frozen in when they were much deeper in the water than when cut out, for so many months' provisions and fuel consumed necessarily lightened them considerably, before the ice was quite through they freed themselves from the remaining ice, and rose a foot or more above the ice which had confined them.

When the ships were fairly afloat, a strict survey of provisions, stores, &c. was made in both; and a full proportion was sent on board us from the Hecla, where they had been stowed for our use. On the 18th the housing over our deck was taken down : but that of the Hecla remained a little longer. Now was seen the utmost activity of all hands, carpenters, sail-makers, armourers, coopers, &c. in examining and repairing whatever belonged to the several departments. The seams of the decks and upper works required much caulking, having been opened by the frost. At the same time our two commanders caused small spots of ground, in sheltered situations, to be prepared as gardens for mustard, cresses, radishes, &c. and the seeds sown. The experiment is well worth trying, and, if we have any success, you shall hear of it : for such, and indeed any fresh vegetables, are the only certain remedies and preventives for the sea-scurvy. Captain Parry continued, nevertheless, to raise his little crops of mustard and cresses in the cabin, where the mildness of the weather greatly favoured their progress.

On the 22d, a party of officers of the Hecla walking some miles westward from the harbour to a hill, the only one in that part of the coast, found a small pool of water from the melted snow, from which they were able to fill a bottle. This was the first time water had been found during the whole time of the ships being in the harbour. The water was mixed with sand, which had promoted its melting; for sand, small stones, pieces of wood, &c. retaining the sun's heat, dissolve the snow and ice round them, whereas the snow itself, being white, repels the heat. The hill now mentioned was called Table-hill, from its appearance, and, although the only conspicuous eminence seen on the coast, does not rise more than one hundred feet above the surrounding plain : the summit is of very small extent, chiefly composed of sand, with fragments of lime-stone, iron-stone, granite, flint, &c. On the 24th we had also, for the first time, two small showers of rain, the one in the morning, the other in the evening. The arrival of these strangers, strangers not only to us but to the climate and country, brought every one on deck to greet them welcome : some held up their faces to receive the kindly drops. I should have mentioned that, in the excursion westward to Table-hill, the excellent anti-scorbutic sorrel was found in abundance, among the tufts of moss growing in moist places. But, at this time the roots only were seen, no leaves having yet appeared; the prospect, however, of soon possessing so valuable a vegetable, gave infinite satisfaction to every member of the expedition.

On the 27th two ivory gulls were observed ; a proof that open water must exist somewhere at no very great distance ; but nothing of that kind could be discovered from any height near the harbour; the whole sea within view, a most discouraging sight for us, appearing still an impenetrable mass of ice, surely not less in thickness than seven or eight feet, as it was round the ships in the harbour. The sea-water in the trenches round the ships, and the little melted pools on the ice remained, however, fluid for the best part of twenty-four hours. In the afternoon of the same day, to our no small surprise, two musquitoes were caught, resembling but smaller than those of warm climates. The wind had, for several days preceding, come from the S. and E S.E., sometimes pretty fresh. These insects had, therefore, been wafted northwards from the woods and marshes on the American continent. The thermometer on the 27th rose to 47° above freezing, and never fell below 32°, or the freezing point. The barometer was at 30 inches. The wind from the southward, light breezes and cloudy weather, all indications of warmth and moisture.

At this time Captain Parry was engaged in measuring a base across the ice, at the mouth of the harbour, and the angles necessary for a survey of the adjoining coast, to be connected with the observations made to the eastward in the beginning of September last year.

The sun being now constantly above the horizon, the temperature of the air moderated, and the people of both ships in good health, it appeared proper to the commander of the expedition to undertake a journey to the interior of the country, which, although principally from conjecture, was supposed to be an island, not connected with any part of the American continent. A number of officers and men of both ships voluntarily offered their services on the occasion, and preparations were made for setting out on Thursday the first of last month. Out of the numerous volunteers, the persons selected were Captain Sabine the astronomer. Messrs. Fisher assistant surgeon, and Nias midshipman, all from the Hecla, and Mr Reid, mishipman of our ship. Serjeants Mac Mahon of the marines, and Martin of the artillery, with three seamen, and two marines, from both ships, together with Captain Parry, made up the number twelve for the expedition. For their accommodation on the journey two tents were prepared, of blankets supported by two pikes used in boarding an enemy's ship, crossed and fastened at each end; a rope stretched between the tops formed the ridge, and large stones laid on the lower part of the blankets on the ground would make a pretty comfortable cover from the snow and wind. A cooking apparatus, fuel, the tents, the provisions, &c. were to be conveyed on a light cart made for the purpose, to be drawn by hand, the whole load weighing about eight hundred pounds. The provisions consisted of the daily allowance of one pound of biscuit, two thirds of a pound of preserved meat, one ounce of salep powder, one ounce of sugar, and half a pint of spirits for each person; and the quantity provided was calculated for a journey of three weeks. Each officer and man had a blanket with drawing-strings at each end to form it into a bag, a pair of spare shoes, two spare pair of stockings, a flannel shirt and a sleeping-cap, for the distinction between night and day had ceased among us. The blankets and clothing each person carried in a knapsack, on his back. The officer's load weighed from seventeen to twenty-four pounds, the men's twenty-four pounds between two, to be carried half a day by turns. The party were provided also with a few fowling-pieces, and pistols, and a considerable quantity of ammunition, to assist in augmenting their stock of provisions if opportunities should offer, and for self defence in case of meeting with animals that might be dangerous.

Into these details I have entered that you may form some notion of the kind of service we may be called on to perform, and the means and mode of performing it. The plan was to proceed directly northward, travelling in what you would call night when the sun is low before us, in order to avoid the glare of the snow, and to rest and sleep in the day when the sun is high behind us for the benefit of the greater warmth. The adventurous party left the ships at five P. M. accompanied by the crews of both ships over the ice to the land, where they parted after three hearty

cheers on both sides. A small number of us however went on
some miles farther carrying the knapsacks and drawing the
baggage-cart; the only things we could do to show the concern
we felt in the success of the expedition and of our shipmates. The
route taken led to the north east hill, because the higher ridges
were the only places the freest from snow; and at eight P. M.
we again gave three hearty cheers: the exploring party went forward to the north and we returned to our ships.

Having thus seen them fairly engaged in their adventurous
enterprise, of which no accounts can be expected until their return to Winter-Harbour, I must resume my notices of our proceedings in that quarter. Here you will naturally be inclined to
ask how the exploratory party are to carry on their various observations, whether astronomical or otherwise. I should have told you
that they are provided with a sextant and artificial horizon, for
determining the latitude and longitude of the different places of
observation; the longitudes are also to be calculated by a pocket
chronometer: other necessary instruments and implements have
also been provided.

Before Captain Parry set out on his over-land expedition he directed our commander, Lieutenant Liddon, and Lieutenant Beechey, the first officer of the Hecla, to use every exertion to prepare
the ships for taking advantage of the first favourable weather for
prosecuting our voyage to the westward. This event it was rather
wished than expected might arrive about the end of last month
or the beginning of this. By that time, judging from the change
in the climate, it was hoped that the ice might break up out at sea,
and consequently what was next to the land might be so far removed from the S. shore of the island, as to permit the ships to
make a good run, or to work their passage to the open sea, which
was supposed to extend from its western extremity.

It was on Friday the 2d of last month that the first flock
of snow-buntings, and the first red phalarope appeared in Winter
Harbour. On the 3d a raven, an arctic gull, and a golden plover
were seen; also a large flock of king-ducks on the wing for the
eastward. The mercury in the thermometer in the shade rose
from + 29° at four A. M. to + 43° at noon, the greatest range that
had been observed in one day, in that part of the scale. Sunday
being the 4th of June, his Majesty's birth-day was celebrated in both ships in the best manner our situation would admit.
Ensigns and pendants were hoisted on board the Hecla, and a
full allowance of provisions was given out to the crews. Ducks
and geese were seen in flocks almost every day coming from the
southward; but these birds, as well as all other game, were soon
frightened away from the ships by our repeated attacks on them
with our fowling-pieces. On the 7th, during a light snow

WINTER DRESS OF OFFICERS AND CREW.

shower, a rainbow appeared, a very rare visitor in these regions, but in all respects like those seen in more temperate climates. On the 9th the first seal was seen lying on the ice, near a hole where he could escape into the water. Musquitoes now appeared in numbers, but they gave us no annoyance. At the same time the buds of the saxifrage and the dwarf willow began to open ; the sorrel was also in flower in some places. On the 11th, some hares were seen to the eastward of the harbour. Some were also seen by a party who returned from the eastward on the 14th, bringing with them three brent-geese or barnacles, six brace of ptarmigans, and a golden plover. On the 14th rein-deer were seen from the ships, for the first time this season: they set off speedily for the northward, having probably but just landed from the ice to the southward.

Thursday 15*th* was a joyful day to us on board ship, for at seven in the afternoon we had the cordial satisfaction of receiving on board Captain Parry and the whole exploratory party from the interior of the island, not only well and hearty, but actually much improved in appearance by their expedition. Having been discovered before they came down to the harbour, every officer and man who could be spared from the ships went out to welcome them, in the most cordial manner. It was highly gratifying to us who had remained with the ships to find the commander entirely satisfied with the progress made in preparing every thing for putting to sea as soon as the ice should afford an opening. Our ship was then nearly ready for sea, but the Hecla was not so forward, as she had a large quantity of ballast to take on board, to supply the weight of the provisions, stores, &c. which had been consumed or sent on board the Griper. The survey of the stores had been completed, and every article of provisions was found to be in as good order as when shipped in the Thames. A little sugar and bread only had contracted some moisture ; and these articles were to be first used. Not only were the provisions chosen of the very best quality, but they had been packed up in strong tight casks which no water could penetrate. It was remarked that not a single rat, mouse, or maggot appeared in any part of the ships.

Friday 16*th*, with the view of collecting as much game as possible whilst we should be detained in Winter Harbour, parties of officers and men were ordered to be prepared from both ships, under Lieutenants Beechey and Hoppner, to remain on the land for some days, and extend their excursions to some distance, which hitherto had not been done. The parties accordingly left the ships this evening with tents, fuel, provisions, &c. Our party, under Lieutenant Hoppner, steered along the coast to the southwestward, with particular orders to report on the state of the sea and ice in that quarter, to which we were to sail. In the forepart of the day a large tent was pitched with a marquee in it, to receive the clocks and other instruments for making observations on the pendulum. In the evening of the 17th our party had the satisfaction to send to the ships the first deer that had been killed in the season, which, when prepared, yielded only sixty pounds of meat. The animal was not of a small size; but being just arrived in the island from probably a long journey over the ice and snow, from the American coast, it was naturally very little in flesh. On the 21st another deer was sent to the ships by our party in the SW. the largest of a herd of fifteen; but after all it afforded not quite eighty pounds of meat. It was so far encouraging to us to discover that the pools on the surface of the ice seemed to be increasing in number and in size: but still no appearance of the breaking up of the ice could be discovered. In the evening of *Thursday* the 29th our party returned from the SW. expedition, with some game, but with what was infinitely more acceptable, the tidings that the ice had been observed in motion off the coast some days before. The noise of the breaking up and crushing of the ice was heard quite loud, although the ice in motion was at least five miles out from the land. It seemed to set eastward at the rate of a mile in the hour. The wind was then moderate, but the day before it blew a fresh gale from the northward. In the course of this excursion a lake was discovered about four miles in circuit, four miles up from the shore, and twelve or fourteen miles to the westward of Winter Harbour. The lake was still frozen over, and might be that which was mentioned by the party who had lost themselves in that quarter in September last.

The party under Lieutenant Beechey returned it seems some days before ours, and reported that the ice was farther advanced in dissolution than at the ships; there being water enough in some places along shore to allow a boat to pass, large rents in the ice were also seen extending a good way outwards. One of that party succeeded in shooting a deer, although the animals were very shy of coming near the tent, by lying down on the ground and imitating the cry of the fawn, which brought the poor animal within gun-shot. Several foxes were seen, having a black spot on each of the hind quarters, the rest of the body being white. One of the party discovered the crown-bone of a whale a mile back from the shore, and at a good height above the water. Before the return of our party from the S.W., in a hole in the ice was found a small fish resembling a whiting: two others of the same kind were soon after found at the same place. No communication was as yet opened from the surface of the ice down to the water, by which those fish could have passed upwards: it is probable that they had been frozen in near the surface of the water, and remained fixed through the winter until now that, the ice beginning to melt, they were again brought to view. In this case, another proof was given of what was formerly observed, that sand, stones, or other solid compact substances, when in a small quantity on ice, by absorbing and retaining warmth from the sun, gradually dissolved the ice under and round them, forming holes which contained the water. On the other hand, a parcel of straw, an open substance containing much empty space, and very unsolid, which had been placed on the ice about the beginning of May, by preventing the action of the sun's rays, hindered the ice under it from melting, which remained elevated a foot above the surface of the ice around it. From this fact, of hollow or porous bodies being bad conductors of heat it is, that straw is employed as a preserver of cold in ice-houses.

I already mentioned that, in a little excursion to Table-hill, to the westward of the harbour, many roots of sorrel were found among the tufts of moss. A fortnight ago the sorrel in the country round the harbour was found to be so forward, that considerable quantities of the leaf might be collected without much trouble; it was consequently ordered that the people from both ships should go on shore in the afternoons, and gather as much as possible of that valuable anti-scorbutic vegetable. It was served out to all without distinction, in the room of our lemon-juice, pickles, &c. and eaten greedily by all on board. To the use of this plant, not forgetting the agreeable exercise obtained in gathering it, we were justified in ascribing the excellent health and spirits possessed, with one exception, by every one belonging to the expedition.

Since the discovery party have returned to their respective ships, I have had much conversation with several of them on their expedition; I have also perused some of the brief journals written from time to time in the course of the journey. I shall, therefore, in my next, give you some notion of what they did and saw, and what they were obliged to undergo; and, in the mean time, I shall leave you to conjecture what mortification it must be for me to write again to you from this wretched quarter of the globe.

Adieu, &c. &c.

LETTER XIII.

Winter Harbour, 1st August, 1820.

ONCE more, my dear Thomas, and for the last time, I do most sincerely pray, you have a letter from me, dated in Winter Harbour. We have long been preparing for our departure; and every thing being now in perfect readiness, we trust the sun will not revisit our northern meridian before we are again under sail.

The paper which accompanies this has been written at different times, as materials could be collected, and as opportunities for committing them to paper occurred. For since my last letter, ot the first of last month, what with real indispensable occupations on board, and what from that restlessness of mind by which other folks, as well as myself, in our little world, are affected, when in the daily, hourly expectation of being set free from our wearisome bondage, if the paper were yet to prepare, prepared by me at the present juncture it could not possibly be.

In perusing this account of the expedition across Melville Island, a name I have never hitherto brought forward, you will naturally be surprised when you meet with the comprehensive term *we*, at the same time that my former communication stated that I was not one of that party. The fact is, that both in conversing with those who were on that expedition, and in reading their travelling notes, *we* came in so frequently and so properly, that it fairly insinuated itself into my memoranda without call, indeed without my being aware of it.

My next letter will probably contain the decision of a most important question: not exactly whether a passage for ships from the Atlantic to the Pacific ocean can be discovered to be practicable at any time of the year, but whether we, at this point of the season, can accomplish such a voyage. We are here in W. long. 110°, and N. lat. 75°. Behring's Strait, the only known opening between the American and the Asiatic continents, is in W long. 170_o. and N. lat. 66°. The direct distance, therefore, across the globe, between these two points, cannot be less than five hundred and fifty leagues. We are now in the beginning of August, and we cannot forget that it cost us no small trouble to cut our way through the ice into this haven, in the latter end of September, after struggling with mighty masses of that substance off the land for many weeks before. That we shall achieve such a work, therefore, in the little remaining ot this season, all circumstances considered, is really more than ought to be expected. In the mean time I return to my Journal, to give you some notices of our proceedings during the month just elapsed.

For some months past the boatswain's mate of the Hecla, William Scott, had been much indisposed, with scurvy and bowel complaint, attended by a general debility of mind as well as of body. On the 27th June he became delirious, and could with difficulty be kept in bed. His malady resisting every antidote which medical aid and humane attention could furnish, early in the morning of *Friday*, the 30th June, Captain Parry was informed that he was not expected to live out the day; but before he could dress to see the unfortunate man he had breathed his last. Scott's disorder bearing appearances unconnected with any circumstances of the expedition, the body was opened, and the result showed that, perhaps, in no country or climate could his life have been long preserved. On *Sunday* the 2d of last month, after divine service in the forenoon, the body was carried on shore, and interred on a level spot of ground at a proper distance back from the beach. The ceremony was conducted with every solemnity required by the occasion, and which our circumstances would permit. The ensigns and pendants of the ships were lowered to half-mast during the funeral procession, which was composed of every officer and man of both ships who could possibly be spared, walking to the grave two and two. A neat tomb-stone was afterwards placed at the head of the grave, facing westward, with a suitable inscription carved on it by Mr. Fisher, assistant-surgeon of the Hecla. The grave was also covered with stone, to prevent its being disturbed by wolves or other animals. In any circumstance the loss of Scott, a very quiet man and an excellent seaman, would have been sufficiently distressing to our little society; but in our forlorn situation in a remote and desolate corner of the world, it was peculiarly affecting. In action the seaman sees his comrades dropping on every side, without much apparent concern; for every instant the lot may be his own; but to see a shipmate carried off by illness in his bed, and be committed to the earth instead of a watery grave, these events have on him a singular effect. Many land folks are deeply averse to the dissection of the dead, especially of their near relations. Among seamen this aversion is particularly strong; and it is an unquestionable proof of the excellent discipline of our expedition, and of the personal respect for the commander entertained by the men, that their companion's body was opened without the least complaint or representation on their part.

In the last days of June the spring tides were uncommonly high, and rising above the ice on the beach made it very difficulty to communicate with the shore. The ice in the harbour was in a state of decay more in fact than in appearance. The winds were mostly from the southward, and the weather cloudy with small rain, and sometimes show; the temperature of the atmosphere was comfortable to our feelings, being always above the freezing point. On the first of July a party came in from the eastward, with a supply of hares, ducks, and grouse. Fifty deer and more had been seen in the course of three days; but in a country wholly destitute of cover it was impossible to get near them. On the same day another fish of the same kind with the former was picked up on the ice; a strong evidence of its progress in dissolution.

In the middle of the month, when the weather was really pleasant to our feelings; for you surely know that feelings of both body and mind are relative; the walks and other exercise ashore, united with the luxuries of game of different sorts, and the plentiful crops of sorrel removed every symptom of scurvy, and placed the crews in as good a state of health and spirits as when they left Europe.

Monday the 17th the mercury in the thermometer rose from 55° to 60°, and continued between these two points from six before to six afternoon. This was the highest point hitherto observed in our journals: for in Melville Island, as in England, the warmest weather always comes after the longest day, just as the coldest weather had been experienced some time after the shortest day. On the 18th a boat could be rowed round the harbour in order to take the soundings, and, as had been before observed, the water was always found to be clear of ice in proportion to its shallowness.

The temperature of the atmosphere now began sensibly to decline; on the 31st the thermometer rose only to 40°: but the whole ice in the harbour appeared to be in motion, although slowly, out to sea. Orders were, therefore, given for embarking the instruments on shore, and instructions were sent by the commander to Lieutenant Liddon, respecting our places of rendezvous when on the future voyage, in case of separation.

At last at eight in the morning of this *Tuesday* the 1st of August, the harbour and bay out as far as Cape Hearne appearing quite free of ice, every thing was got on board, and at 1 P. M. both ships weighed and ran joyfully out of the harbour. But here I must lay aside my pen for the present.

Remaining, &c.

Notes on the Journey from Winter Harbour, across Melville Island, to the Sea on the North Coast, and the return by a different Track.

THURSDAY, the 1st of *June*, 1820, at five in the afternoon, we left the ships, and going round the bottom of the harbour, where they lay, directed our route on an easy ascent to North-east Hill, so called because it is situated in that direction from the station of the ships, above a mile off. In a generally low country this hill, although not two hundred and fifty feet above the sea, forms an object of some note; and it was only on the heights and ridges where the ground was clear of snow. Taking leave of our companions from the ships at 8 P. M., we proceeded over a plain, on which the snow was luckily so hard, that our cart went easily along, till 11 P. M., when we halted for *dinner*. For as we purposed to travel in what we called the night, to avoid injury to the sight from the glare of the snow in the full sun; and to repose in the day, when we should have the benefit of what warmth his beams might excite in us and in the air, our hours of meals were reversed, and what in other circumstances might have been a fashionable supper, became with us a most unfashionable dinner.

Our halting place was close on the N. side of three small eminences of sand-stone and sand. The soil here seemed more fertile than near the harbour, producing sorrel, dwarf willow, and naked poppy. The poor willows, however, could not afford as much dry wood as would liquefy the snow for our meal, we were therefore obliged to trench upon our slender stock of fuel, an article we could but ill spare.

A little farther on we discovered a level extent of snow in which even with a glass not a spot of free ground was seen. It seemed to be bounded by a range of hills, at times seen during walks into the country from Winter Harbour, and from their atmospherical colour called the Blue Hills. This Plain precisely resembled an inlet of the sea, or a lake covered with ice and snow: but it was probably from three hundred to four hundred above the water At half-past six A.M. halted and pitched our tents on the hardest spot we could find, which, nevertheless, became quite soft as the day advanced. Here we killed 3½ brace of grouse, and saw two deer, the first this season. With them was a fawn that must have been the produce of the island; but they were too shy for us. At seven A. M. in the shade, the mercury stood at 34°, and this was the last observation made with the thermometer, which was here accidentally and unfortunately broken.

At five P. M. struck our tents and proceeded on our journey northwards, after fixing the latitude and longitude of our position.

Halting for dinner and rest at eleven P. M. we again pushed forward on Saturday the third, crossing a ravine or two running from ENE. to WSW. in them much snow but no water. Captain Parry and Captain Sabine having passed on before the rest of the company, to point out the easiest track, sat down to wait for us. While there a rein-deer trotted up to them and continued playing round them for a quarter of an hour, not more than thirty or forty yards off. This was on the N. side of a ravine; and the deer hearing our noise on the S. side came over boldly to us, where his curiosity and confidence in us were rewarded with some shots, but without effect. On this he crossed back to the gentlemen he had first accosted, going still nearer to them than before. They rose up and went on, and the poor fellow bore them company as a dog would have done; trotting on to some distance, and then trotting back within forty or fifty yards of them. Halting at six A. M. to observe the latitude and longitude he staid by them till we came near, when he again trotted off and disappeared. When he was about to set off he always reared on his hind legs like a goat as in play, and then scampered away. In this day's progress the soil, a composition of decayed vegetables and sand, produced abundantly saxifrage and sorrel. The fore-part of the day was foggy, and about six P. M. came to a gully perhaps one hundred feet deep, over which it cost an hour's labour to convey our baggage waggon. The stones we met with were all sandstone but when bruised by our wheels they gave a smell like that of fetid limestone: no limestone however did we see. In the sandstone were inserted pieces of coal of a slaty kind which burned but badly.

Sunday 4th June, continued still northward, as well as we could judge, over the same unvaried plain, where the glare of the snow and sun was most painful to the eyes, with only a small patch here and there where we might hope to meet with water, and where alone we could encamp. A gale coming away from the SSE. our seamen, mindful of their profession, as they did on the ice in the canal for the ships in the harbour, now rigged out a tent-blanket as a sail on the cart, which proved of essential service in helping us on before the wind. The drift had so covered the ground that with difficulty could a patch be found free from snow large enough to receive our tents. In all this day's march no animals were seen, only some fox-tracks, nor the least visible vegetation. The gale and drift increasing we remained till seven P. M. in the tents, now for the first time not over comfortable from the beating of the wind and snow. They however afforded sufficient cover from the storm, having the cart tilted up to windward. When closely wrapped up in our blanket-bags, our fatigue in dragging the cart, in which every one of the party took his share, procured us refreshing sleep. The wind now veering to SW. the weather became milder, and we continued our march, placing the men's knapsacks on the cart to render them fitter to drag it along. One sail was hoisted when we set out; but as the wind now, as the seamen said, was on our larboard quarter, they rigged out a second blanket as a main-sail, an operation which afforded them amusement as well as relief in their toil. The dinner of the 4th of June thus came round in the morning of the 5th, but in both tents we did not fail to drink very cordially the health of our venerable sovereign George III. Between the fog and the glare of the snow it was with no little difficulty that we kept the course projected northwards. Our practice was to follow the two persons who went on before the cart party; and they laying a compass on the snow and comparing the bearings with the known place of the sun at the different hours, chose some object at a distance on which to lead the march. So thick however was the fog, and so deceiving is the view of objects over a plain surface of bright snow, that what we conceived to be at a considerable distance often turned out to be very close at hand. Then the labour of determining our course by the compass was to be repeated. While in this embarrassing situation, at 8 A. M. a line of dark clear ground appeared right before us. This turned out to be the northern edge of a ravine sixty feet or more in depth, and some hundred yards in breadth. Passing over it we encamped on the N. bank, having effected less than two miles in the morning, from the softness and dampness of the snow, which made it next to impossible to get forward the cart. The ravine was covered with blocks of sandstone, under which we found sweet water in plenty. Taking the opportunity to cook our grouse here we fared sumptuously and went to rest. By a meridian altitude of the sun the latitude of our station was found to be $75° 22' 43''$, and its longitude by the chronometer $111° 14' 26''$. Our progress hitherto in a straight line must therefore be only about thirty-six miles in a direction a little to the westward of north.

Resuming our march at half-past five P. M. with clear weather and a fine breeze from the southward, all sail was set on the cart as soon as it was got out of the ravine. During this march several of the party were attacked by snow-blindness; very painful while in motion, but generally relieved at the halt by the usual cooling applications and some hours' rest. Travelling over another snowy plain several miles, without a single object of interest or variety, or any animal of any kind being seen, but some tracks of deer and foxes being observed, we arrived on an eminence a little before midnight, from whence some dark-coloured ground was perceived towards the NE., beyond which appeared higher land at a considerable distance. Between them appeared a broad level snowy plain, or perhaps an arm of the sea covered with ice. To the westward the Blue Hills were still in sight distant probably about four leagues.

Here we had a proof how liable to error must be the account of a journey of several hundred miles in a climate so far, and even not so far to the northward as our position, founded wholly on estimated courses and distances, without any astronomical observations. This liability to error must be particularly considered in examining the route described by Hearne, in his journey to the northern sea of America from the settlements on the W. coast of Hudson's Bay; for in a course of many hundred miles of that journey not a single observation of latitude and longitude, or of the variation of the compass, was obtained.

Thursday 6th, The sharp frosty wind from the SSE. roused us from our tents at 4 A. M. and travelling on about half a mile in half an hour northwards, arrived on the summit of a hill which commanded a view of the broad level plain, or frozen inlet of the sea already mentioned. The high land beyond it now plainly appeared to be a separate country or island. The hill, probably, towards five hundred feet above the level of the sea, descended rapidly for two-thirds of its height, and then extended much more gently for some miles, to what we now began to think was not land, but the frozen sea to the northward and north-east. The hill we halted on was covered with masses of sand-stone, over which we had great difficulty in forcing our carriage. The plain below us, which seemed unbounded on the north-west and south-east between our position and the high land to the north-east appeared, in every respect, when viewed by the telescope, like the frozen sea on the south side of the island; the surface shewing many pools of water, and ranges of mounds of ice collected along the beach. In order to remove all doubts respecting the nature of this frozen plain, the party descended to within a couple of miles of the shore, when heavy clouds coming away from the south-east, soon sent down a fall of sleet and snow. To prevent being wet, in a situation where no means of drying ourselves existed, a piece of dry ground was sought out for the tents; at 6 A. M. they were pitched, und. r the lee of a wall which was raised to the height of six feet, to defend us from the wind, now very strong.

The wind continuing to blow fresh, and the ground covered with deep snow, the tents were not struck: but at 6 P. M. Captain Parry, with Messrs. Nias and Reid, midshipmen, and a quarter-master of our ship, set off to examine the plain to the northward. Travelling to the westward of N. for nearly two miles through very deep snow, principally from the day's fall, they came to ice forced upon the beach, with a number of rents parallel to the shore, and, probably, occasioned by the rise and fall of the tide. We had so long been accustomed to this in Winter Harbour, that we could not well be mistaken. Proceeding westward for a couple of miles along the shore, they gained a point of land from eighty to one hundred feet above the level of the sea, which commanded an extensive view, and presented large irregular masses or hummocks of ice thrown up by the floes on the sea all along as far as could be seen. These exactly resembled the masses or bergs, as we call them, under which we had often found security on the south coast of the island. Returning to the tents the whole party dined, and at $1\frac{1}{2}$ A. M. of *Wednesday the 7th*, removed, and encamped on the elevated point just mentioned. It froze in the shade all the day, and a fresh breeze from the northward rendered it very cold in the tents, although pitched under the lee of the ice-bergs on the beach. The water seen on the ice was now solid ice, and some of our canteens burst in freezing. The weather, fortunately, cleared up about noon, when observations were made to establish the position of the point in north lat. $75_{\circ}\ 34'\ 47''$, and west long. $110_{\circ}\ 35'\ 52'$, so that now we were $12'\ 18''$ to the eastward of N. from Winter Harbour, distant forty-eight miles. The variation of the compass $135° 03' 55''$ easterly.

Being satisfied that the high land beyond the sea before us was detached from that where we were, the commander called it Sabine Island, the north-west point of which, a bluff headland, he named Cape Mudge, and the most remote point at the extremity of the Blue Hills was called Cape Fisher, bearing nearly north-west from our place of observation, the land between them sweeping round in a deep bay. The high point of observation was called Point Nias, and the most remote point of our own island, bearing east by south, was named Point Reid. Sabine Island appeared to extend north-west and south-east. Out to the northward of Point Nias ran a continued range of ice hummocks for between two and three miles, clearly pointing out that they had grounded on a reef of rocks under water. The effect of this has been, that the ice along the shore, all the way eastward to Point Reid, seems never to have been crushed by the floes out at sea; while to the westward, for perhaps eight leagues to Cape Fisher, the beach is lined with icebergs, evident proofs of enormous pressure by fields of ice in irresistible motion.

It was 10 P. M. before we succeeded in digging a hole through the ice under Point Nias, which was found to be no less than fourteen feet four inches in thickness, far exceeding that of any floes we had ever seen. The water took three quarters of an hour in rising in the hole to the proper level, within fifteen inches of the surface of the ice. It did not taste very salt being mixed, no doubt, with dissolved ice broken by our pikes in digging the hole: but it was so salt as to satisfy every one that we had reached the sea, and a canteen was filled with it to be examined on the return of the party to the ships.

The country along this northern coast of our island is as barren as land can be : not a single hardy poppy to be seen, nothing but a few tufts of stunted moss and lichen. The constant sandstone was varied by only a few pieces of red granite, and red and white feldspar, discovered after a search of several hours. The sandstone whitish and slaty. That the sea here is not always covered with floes of ice is probable, from the discovery of two pieces of drift-wood, both of pine, seventy or eighty yards back from the icebergs, on a spot at least twenty feet above the present surface of the sea. The one $7\frac{1}{2}$ feet long, and about 3 inches in thickness; the other much smaller. They were mostly buried in the sandy soil, and must have been there a long time, for, on being handled, they separated into fibres the length of the grain. As Point Nias was to be the most northern point of our expedition, for there we had come upon the open sea, and assured ourselves that Melville Island was really insulated, we resolved to bring back some tokens of our achievement: but nothing could we collect but a few fragments of the granite beforementioned.

Thursday 8th—Having dined at midnight, the tents were packed up, and the cart drawn up to the summit of Point Nias soon after 2 A. M. There was constructed a monument to preserve the memory of our arrival on the spot. This monument was of stones, of which there was no want on the ground, piled up in a rude cone twelve feet in diameter, and twelve feet in perpendicular height. In the centre was formed a small chamber to contain a tin cylinder, inclosing a slip of parchment, on which was written a short account of the party and the expedition. With it were deposited a sixpence of 1817, a penny-piece of 1797, and a halfpenny of 1807 : the men would also contribute their mite, by adding some naval uniform buttons to the stock.

Having thus taken formal possession of the northernmost point of our progress over Melville Island, so named from the present First Lord of the Admiralty, and seeing nothing more to be done, promising any utility to the expedition, it was resolved to return to Winter Harbour, taking another route more to the westward, both to avoid the miserable tracts we had already traversed, and by ascending the Blue Hills to obtain a more extended view of the western parts of the island and of the sea in that direction. Those hills seemed to run, in general, north and south; they could not, therefore, draw us much out of our proper line of march: we had, besides, abundance of provisions, should we be detained a few days beyond the time first proposed; for our stock was calculated for the consumption of three weeks, although it was not intended to continue so long absent from the ships.

Travelling in a direction a very little to the southward of W. along an elevated ridge on the coast, to avoid the snow which lay very deep in the lower grounds, at $7\frac{1}{4}$ P. M. encamped close to a hillock on fine sandy ground, which afforded the softest and driest bed we had had in the whole journey. The hillock composed of earth covered with moss was full of foxes'· or more probably of hares' burrows like a rabbit-warren. To procure some fresh food we tried to smoke them out, but none appeared: nor did a single hare ever come in our way on our route.

Resuming our journey at $5\frac{1}{2}$ P. M. to the SW. crossed a snowy plain $1\frac{1}{2}$ mile in breadth, and stretching from the sea on the N. as far as the eye could reach in the opposite direction. Proceeding in all 5 miles, we began to ascend the Blue Hills; but their most elevated parts seemed to be still ten or twelve miles farther to the westward. Halting for dinner at midnight we continued our march still to the SW. following a course very irregular but the most agreeable we had pursued, on account of the unevenness of the ground. At the end of a quarter of a mile came to a stream of running water, the first seen this season. The sun softening the snow and melting the ice on the pools, made walking very laborious and inconvenient. Passed by some deers' horns, killed three ptarmigans, and a pair of ducks: a pair of bank-swallows, as it was said, were seen by one of the people. Proceeding over a succession of heights and swampy hollows and ravines, which made it very bad walking and difficult to get along the cart, we were obliged to halt about 11 P. M. having advanced not more than 4 miles. Starting again between 2 and 3 A. M. of Saturday the 10th, travelled till past 7 over hills and plains intersected by ravines, in which our cart sunk up to the naves.

The weather was extremely severe during our march and in the night, but the wind veering round to the northward in the morning of Sunday the 11th, started again at four o'clock. After great labour in transporting our cart over a ravine with high steep banks, we found ourselves on higher ground than before. Proceeding for four miles over this elevated plain, at the southern extremity broke in upon us a prospect at once picturesque and magnificent. This view descended from a height of probably towards nine hundred feet perpendicular, to a spacious plain of ice, unbounded to the westward for 5 or 6 leagues, the view to the eastward intercepted by other high grounds. The fog which covered the plain being opened up by the wind we discovered a rocky island in the middle. Coming to a ravine which terminated at the frozen plain we found it of very difficult access. The sides which were exceedingly steep were covered with blocks of sandstone of all sizes, and yet over them we found that we must certainly descend to the bottom. This was attempted; but in a pass which the best-constructed carriage could not long stand, it is no wonder if our awkward cart soon gave way; and when it was got about half way down the bank, all at once our axle-tree broke over in the middle. The baggage was therefore unloaded and carried down to the bottom, where we encamped a little before noon, in north latitude 75° 12′ 50″, and in west longitude by chronometer 111° 50′ 05″. The variation of the magnetic needle 125° 12′ 22″ easterly. The wind being high from NNW, and the weather cold and raw, a wall was built to windward of the tents, to supply the place of our unfortunate cart, which, when tilted, used to afford tolerable shelter. The whole party being a good deal fatigued, the halt was lengthened till near midnight, and then all were employed in dividing and sorting the baggage, so as to carry it on during the remainder of the journey. When this arrangement was made, in which every one, officer and man, was to carry his fair proportion, and which every person excepting one, certainly not the chief person of the party, most cheerfully undertook to carry, it was happily discovered that the loss of the cart was not much to be regretted. The ground was so swampy, and wet or rugged, that it would have been almost impracticable to drag it forward, and our progress must of course have been greatly retarded.

Monday 12th, part of the light frame of the cart being employed as fuel, we cooked our grouse and supped with a delight which can be conceived by those only who have experienced what it is to have a warm meal after so long exposure to cold and wet, with no other comfort than preserved meats in what might be called a frozen state. Proceeding eastward along the shore to a point advancing into the bay, the rocks overhanging the beach, consisting of the usual sand-stone, were so shattered and steep as to have more the appearance of ruined buildings than of natural cliffs. The adjoining cove, called after Mr. Bushnan, midshipman of the Hecla, was undoubtedly the most pleasant and habitable spot met with in all our voyage in the arctic regions. It is sheltered from the bitterest winds, and well situated for game. Grass, moss, dwarf-willow, and saxifrage are more plentiful than in any other place we had seen in the island, and a ranunculus was met with in full flower.

Arriving at the point at 5 A. M. the gulf or inlet seemed to extend a good way eastward, near probably to our northward track, it was resolved to cross it over the ice, dividing the journey, by steering first for the island in the middle, which we reached after walking 5 miles at 7 A. M. Landing at the SE. part of the island, which Captain Parry named after Mr. Hooper, purser of the Hecla, one of the men going to drink from a little pool on the surface found it sufficiently salt. The tents were pitched under the highest part of the island, which rises nearly perpendicular about seven hundred feet: a commanding view of the gulf was taken with the glass; and it was named Liddon's Gulf, after the commander of the Griper. From 5 to 7 leagues westward it seemed to terminate at two headlands, to be named after Lieutenants Beechey of the Hecla, and Hoppner of the Griper: the former cape bearing from the island S. 86° W., and the latter S. 65° W: The north coast of the gulf being the southern termination of the Blue Hills, is much more elevated and precipitous than the south coast. Hooper's Island consists of the usual stratified sandstone; but on the summit appeared a great deal of clay ironstone of various shades, from deep brown to dark blue. Pieces of calcareous spar were found on the beach. The lat. is 75° 05′ 18″, the long. 111° 56′ 58″, variation of the needle 123° 47′ 58″

Remaining in this barren spot till 6 P. M. we set out on the ice, on which the snow was so softened by the sun that, loaded as we were, we sunk up to the knees, and after much labour got to the land at half past 8, having walked only $3\frac{1}{2}$ miles. On landing saw two deer, but too shy for our purpose, and took our course to south-east along a bank between the gulf, and a small lagoon communicating with it. On this bank found the root and a yard length of a small pine-tree, fifteen feet above the present level of the sea. Found, also, the skeleton of a musk-ox fast frozen into the ground, and the horns of rein-deer. The soil here is rich, producing abundantly fine moss, grass, saxifrage, and poppy. From different marks this spot seemed to be a favourite feeding place for musk-oxen, deer, and hares. Halted at $11\frac{1}{2}$ P. M. the night very clear and fine; and remained a day in the hope of obtaining specimens of the different animals inhabitants of the island.

Tuesday 13*th*, our sportsmen were early out, and had a shot at a musk-ox feeding, but without apparently wounding him, on which he set off at a smart space over the hills. This animal is, in appearance, very ill-proportioned, for the hair of his body descends so low, that the legs seem to be only a few inches in length; and, from what was found from time to time in his track, it is evident that, when running, he treads upon the hair at almost every step: he, nevertheless, gets over the ground with much more speed than would be expected. In the pursuit he frequently tore up the ground with his horns, turning round occasionally to face, but never to attack, his pursuers. A herd of twelve deer were also seen, of which three only, by much the largest, had horns, with which they pushed forward the others when attempting to stop. The birds observed were brent-geese, or barnacles, ptarmigans, plovers, boatswains, and snow-buntings; several field-mice, of the kind called Hudson's Bay mice, were seen and two caught. All over the island the holes and tracks of these little creatures were occasionally seen. One of them being pursued, and finding no hole near, turning round set himself against a stone, and bit the finger of the person who laid hold of him.

These animals, it appeared, were not the only kind of inhabitants of this favoured spot; for, on a point of land nearly a mile to the westward of the tents, and within a hundred yards of the beach, were found the ruins of six huts, once occupied by Esquimaux from the North American continent. They exactly resembled the huts seen in the end of August last on Byam Martin Island, as well as those discovered in Captain Ross's expedition of 1818, on the west coast of Greenland in Baffin's Bay. These huts formed irregular circles, or oblongs, of rough stones five or six feet one way, by eight the other; the walls only about two feet in height. The pavement consisted of flags of sandstone, and was overgrown with moss, as were the walls with lichen: but in what number of years such growth may be produced we have no way to ascertain. On one side of each hut was a small projection, perhaps the place for storing provisions, and near one of the huts was an inclosed place two or three feet square, which was, probably, the fire or cooking-place, for the marks of fire were visible on the stones.

At 4 P.M. a breeze came on from the south with a fall of snow, and as we were setting out a herd of deer appeared, but we obtained none of them. Our intention was to steer in that direction till we came in sight of Table Hill, situated about five miles to the westward of Winter Harbour: but as we began to get wet from the sleet, we halted at 8 P.M., the wind coming away strong from the south-east quarter; and the night turned out very boisterous.

Wednesday 14*th*, the weather clearing up, got again under way soon after 4 A. M., and crossed several eminences which commanded a good prospect of the rocky steep cliffs down which we had come in arriving at Liddon's Gulf. Some ravines, also, ran across our route from north-east to south-west. At last getting sight of Table Hill we pushed forward for that point, and halted at 8 A. M., pitching our tents on a spot of dry ground on the bank of a ravine; a great part of the country round seeming to be free from snow. The only birds seen were the snow-buntings, which hovered round the tents, like sparrows, all the time we halted. It had been formerly remarked, that the surface of the Table Hill, like all the country we had traversed, consisted of sandstone, having on it many masses of lime-stone of different colours; we were, therefore, attentive to discover where the lime-stone began; but none appeared until within a few hundred yards of the hill, where some small pieces were found, mixed with granite and feldspar, scattered on the surface of the sandy soil. Halting at the foot of the Table Hill, about 10 A. M., we waited till noon to ascertain the position of the highest point by observation. It was found to be in N. lat. 74° 48′ 33″, and W. long. 111° 1·1′ 49″, the variation of the compass 123° 05′ 30″ easterly. The most easterly of the Table Hills, for there are two eminences, is the most remarkable object in that part of Melville Island; the people were, therefore, set to work to collect stones for a monument, the better to point out the harbour in which the ships lay, should any vessel ever pass that way and be in want of a safe station. This monument was round and conical, ten feet in diameter at the base, and between ten and eleven feet in perpendicular height. In the centre was deposited a piece of parchment with the date and the names of the ships; but a sloping passage was left at the bottom, through which a copper case can be introduced, to be prepared when we get to the ships, containing a full account of the expedition. After finishing this monument the party rested till past 3 P. M., when, having the mortification to discover no opening in the sea to the westward, we marched on to Winter Harbour, and arrived well and hearty on board our respective ships at seven in the evening.

LETTER XIV.

Baffin's Bay, 1st September, 1820.

AT last, my dear Thomas, we have closed the multiplied dangers of the narrow seas: we are now again in a branch of the great northern ocean, and on our way for Old England. Of the various and contradictory feelings by which all on board were agitated, before the resolution to relinquish the attempt to prosecute our intended voyage to the westward was adopted, it would be idle in me to give you a statement. If a due consideration of the situation in which we were placed, previously to our coming to that mortifying determination, be insufficient to convince you and other friends at home not only of its propriety but of its absolute necessity, for me to imagine that any thing in my power to say could have a greater effect would be the height of presumption. I now therefore return to the details of our proceedings during the month just elapsed.

My last letter stated that having taken on board all the instruments employed on shore, for astronomical or other purposes, and the ice being sufficiently open, at one P. M. of *Tuesday* 1st *August*, we weighed anchor and stood out of Winter Harbour. We entered it on *Friday*, the 24th of *September* last year: we consequently passed in that desolate and dreary station upwards of ten long months. Our proper discovery-voyage was of still longer duration; for the very day of our deliverence from imprisonment in Melville Island was the anniversary of our passing from Baffin's Bay into Sir James Lancaster's Sound, of which little more than the entrance had been formerly explored.

Having cleared the points of Winter Harbour and the ice-hummocks off Cape Hearne, in $6\frac{1}{4}$ fathoms of water, we had the gratification to observe the coast of Melville Island to the south-westward, the direction of our course, much clearer of ice that had been expected, and than it was a month later when we were here last year. The late winds off the land from W. and NW. had driven the ice four or five miles out from the shore; and the small fragments floating in the channel were not of such a size or weight as to give much interruption to our navigation; for the fair-way was in breadth from 1 to $2\frac{1}{2}$ miles, as far as could be discovered to the westward from the mast-head. On rounding Cape Hearne the wind drew more to the westward than in Winter Harbour, which, with the necessary operations to keep clear of floating ice, rendered our navigation slow and tedious. We had also to contend with a current or tide to the eastward, which, as it stopped about 7 P. M. was supposed to be the flood-tide; for high-water in Winter-Harbour would be about $7\frac{1}{2}$ P. M.

During our preparations for sea on board the Griper, the commander adopted and introduced every improvement which was practicable, to correct the known defects of the ship in sailing. But the original defects in her construction and rigging were, in our circumstances, incurable. The consequence was that, when we got out of the harbour, she sailed and worked in some respects worse than before, although we had a fine working breeze and smooth water, just the situation in which she used to make the best way. From this it happened that at midnight the Hecla, which had got eight miles to the westward of us was obliged to ly-to; for the weather becoming hazy and the open channel wider than before, there was danger of our parting company. At three A. M. of the 2d, having joined the Hecla, both proceeded to the westward. In the morning our commander received a letter from Captain Parry, desiring to have a particular account of the state of the Griper, that if found incurable, the ship's company, provisions,

&c. should be removed into the Hecla, and the voyage be prosecuted in that ship alone.

About noon the wind coming away from SSW. a heavy floe of ice closed in on the shore, and the ships found a convenient spot behind some heavy grounded ice, our ship touching the beach, that the Hecla might have room to lie without us. Soon after we had made fast a bear was heard growling near our ship, but we did not get sight of him. This was the second animal of that kind that came near us since we arrived on the coast of Melville island; the first was on the 1st of *October*, soon after our entrance into Winter Harbour. In this place the men of both ships went ashore to gather sorrel, which was found in abundance, but rather too old for use, having lost its acid juices.

At noon of the 4th, the wind having come round to the eastward of N. the heavy ice moved off from the land, and near midnight we gained to the westward to Cape Providence, the place where our Greenland master and his party were restored on board from their very dangerous situation on shore, on the 13th *September* last year. The coast here being lofty and precipitous, the water was deep, and notice could take the ground to afford any shelter amongst it, in the case of the outward floes closing in on the land. We were therefore anxious to push on westward, and had just got far enough to see the channel quite clear at the supposed extreme point of the island, when the wind failed, and we could make little or no way. Here again we had sight of what had been so often taken for land to the southward, still under the same appearance as before. As the ice never moved off above five or six miles from the shore, this seemed to strengthen the notion that its motion was stopped only by bearing on some land to the southward.

At noon of the 5th, Captain Parry and some gentlemen of the Hecla landed near one of the deep and broad ravines with which the western part of Melville Island is broken down. The height of the cliffs was measured, nearly 850 feet, composed of sandstone and clay ironstone. While they were on shore a breeze from the eastward brought us up with the Hecla, and her party returning on board, both ships stood again to the westward. In a short time, however, the ice was found to be close in with the land at Cape Hay: the Hecla therefore chose a position in seven fathoms water, not more. than 20 yards from the beach, which was lined all round the point with masses of ice of great size and weight, forced upon the ground by the prodigious pressure of the floes out at sea. We were considerably to the eastward at this time, and by signal from the Hecla, also made fast at a point two or three miles from her.

In sailing along the shore this evening the cliffs presented the appearance of a high artificial wall, the resort of vast flocks of birds. On going ashore to collect some specimens of them, the apparent wall was found to consist of horizontal beds of sandstone, in all about thirty feet high, of which the more solid parts had resisted the weather, while the softer parts had been consumed, thus forming the appearance of a decayed wall. Here prodigious numbers of gulls and other sea-fowl lodged secure from every enemy but man; and so firmly did they defend their young that until some shots were fired it was not safe to approach their seats.

On the morning of the 7th a black whale appeared close by the Hecla, the only fish of that sort since the 22d of last August. An officer who went on shore to have a view of the ice to the westward brought a very discouraging report, for not a single opening or hole was to be seen in the ice for many miles to the westward. Land was however discovered with the glass in the shape of three capes between WSW. and SSW: but the loom or faint appearance of land extended to SE. The distance of the capes was supposed to be from 40 to 50 miles. Here a fawn was shot, yielding nearly 40 pounds of venison, and plenty of sorrel, fine and well grown, and retaining much more acid than any lately gathered.

On the 8th, Captain Parry went ashore to have a view of the ice and of the land beyond it, which he estimated to be from 50 to 55 miles off. The three capes, or perhaps three hills, seemed to be situated in W. long. 117° or more, being the westernmost land yet discovered in the sea on the north of the American continent: this extensive tract of country was named Banks's Land, from respect to the President of the Royal Society.

Wednesday, 9th August—The ice has been almost constantly in motion for some days, in opposite directions, but never so clear as to allow the ships to proceed westward. Two pieces of ice came in contact with one another near the ships, about 10 P. M., and one of them, above 40 feet in thickness, and three times as much in length and breadth, was forced quite up on its edge on the other piece. What, then, must be the fate of a ship, were she as strong as wood and iron can make her, if brought into such a situation between two floes, or between a floe and the shore! This last consideration rendered the position of our ships by no means secure or comfortable.

This same day our hunters have been particularly fortunate, for they have at last seen and shot a musk-ox. He was going along shore eastwards, and so confined, by the nature of the ground, that he passed within shot from the ships. It did not appear, however, that he was wounded, for on hearing the report he galloped off much more quickly than could have been expected from his make. Coming at last to a spot where he must either have taken to the ice on the beach, or made his way up the steep cliff, and seeing himself attacked so closely that he could not escape, he placed himself in front of a large rock, where no other animal could annoy him. There facing his pursuers, he prepared for defence; but against our sportsmen he had no security; he therefore soon fell into our hands. His length from the snout to the tail, was six feet seven inches, and the tail three inches. Height from the fore-hoof to the top of the shoulder, four feet eight inches. Fore-leg two feet three inches; hind-leg two feet nine inches. From hind hoof to top of the back, four feet two inches. End of snout to fore shoulder, two feet five inches. Distance between tips of horns, which are curiously bent down like hooks, on each side of the head, two feet. Circumference of neck, close to the head, three feet eight inches. Length of longest hair on the rump, two feet five inches. Weight of the whole estimated above 700 pounds: but that of the eatable carcase 420 pounds. When brought on board, the carcase smelled very strongly of musk, as did the whole of the meat more or less, especially the heart. The meat was remarkably fat, and, when hung up in quarters, looked as well as any English beef. It was served out to both ships in the place of salt provisions, and, notwithstanding the musky flavour, much relished by almost every one on board: as was the flesh of a young seal, killed by the people of our ship, which was tender and very palatable, although not very pleasing to the eye, being of a dirty red colour. The muskox had a thick mane, reaching from the head to the bunch on the shoulders, of a pale russet colour. Behind the mane was a saddle of whitish short hair, extending a foot and a half along the ridge of the back. The legs to the knees whitish, and the hair like that of the English ox. Under the long hair was a very fine sort of an ash-colour, capable of making cloth equal to that of English wool. From certain appearances it is probable that the animal casts this wool every year. The hair on his brow, and the roots of the horns, were covered and matted with earth, from his practice, of which we witnessed, of tearing up the ground with his head when attacked. All things considered, the musk-ox must be a very formidable antagonist, even to the polar bear himself.

I already mentioned that a mass of ice forced up on another piece, was above forty feet in thickness. An immense floe, which chiefly opposed our passage to the westward, was about seven feet above the water; and, taking this to be one-seventh part of the whole, its thickness must have been above fifty feet. The surface was, besides, covered with many eminences, giving it the appearance of hill and dale, and of them some were at least twenty feet above the surface of the floe; the thickness in those places about seventy feet, was much greater than that of any ice we had before seen. According to our Greenlandmen on board, this ice greatly resembled that on the coasts of Spitzbergen and East Greenland, but much more solid : on the Spitzbergen ice the snow was said to be much deeper than with us.

From every thing we could observe, the sea at the W. end of Melville Island seemed to have something particular in its nature; for this year in August, and last year in September, we found it to be equally obstructed by ice, and wholly inaccessible for shipping. The winds off the land, which farther eastward used to drive off the ice for several miles from the shore, in this western part had no effect on it. The easterly winds had blown fresh for the best part of two days, and yet the ice, now of prodigious thickness and compactness, had not moved a foot. Hence it appeared that, still farther to the westward, in the sea beyond Melville Island, no open clear spaces existed, into which the ice, where we lay, could be driven. Here, therefore, all navigation westward became impracticable,

Friday 11*th*, some officers of the Hecla ascended a hill over the beach, where the ships were made fast to the grounded ice : but they could descry no opening of any kind in the ice, or between it and the shore. The height of this hill was about 800 feet, and the nearest hills behind it may be 200 feet more; making the highest land in the western portion of Melville Island, about 1000 feet in perpendicular height.

Monday 14*th*, Mr. Fisher, one of the surgeons of the Hecla, made an experiment to ascertain the specific gravity of the ice round the ship. Forming a cube out of a solid piece of floe, of 14·7 inches a side, and placing it in a vessel of salt-water, at the temperature of 34°, and of the gravity of 1·0105, 1·8 inch remained above the water, and 12·9 inches below it; that is, very nearly one-eighth part of the whole mass. Experiments on the ice to the eastward showed, that in general one-seventh of the whole remained above the surface; the ice there was, of course, less solid than that to the westward.

For these several days past the masses of ice had been close upon the ships, in consequence of very fresh gales from the eastward ; and, as the ships were wholly exposed to the floes, preparations were made for both taking the beach in the most advantageous manner, that, if possible, the largest vessel might be preserved. Our principal defence was from the loose pieces of thick ice, which drew so much water as to ground before they touched us, and so served as excellent fenders to keep off the otherwise irresistible shock of the external floes.

At 11 P. M. of *Saturday* the 12*th*, the ice closed in so much on our ship, as to force her against a tongue of ice projecting from the land under the surface, and to raise her stern two feet out of the water. By this force she cracked a good deal, and must have received a twist, but no bad effects were observed to follow it. At first she heeled or leant over towards the land, but, on being forced higher up on the tongue, she fell over outwards to the deep water. In this situation our commander ordered all journals and other papers of importance to be secured, and prepared every thing for saving the provisions and stores, and, in fact, whatever articles were of value in the prospect of shipwreck, which we now hourly expected. Here we were sensible of the judiciousness of Captain Parry's instruction for keeping the vessels at some distance from one another, as the best security we could have for preserving at least one of them. The Hecla, which was separated from us by a point of land, as we found afterwards, was in the near prospect of being driven into a similar situation; and her preservation as the largest, the stoutest, and the best sailer of the two, became the object of chief consideration with the people of both. In the afternoon the ice having slackened, the Griper righted, having received no other injury than splitting her rudder. Early in the morning of the 14th, the ice pressed on the Hecla so hard, as to give her a heel or inclination of a foot and a half; but in a few hours the pressure diminished, and she righted without any perceptible injury.

The view from the neighbouring heights displayed nothing in our track to the westward but one continued compact immense extent of ice. This, combined with the state of the winds, confirmed more and more the opinion of the commander and the principal officers of the expedition, that to procure a passage along the southern coast of Melville Island was wholly impossible. The next resource was to stand out to sea, and endeavour to discover a passage by the southward. In consequence of this resolution, and the wind coming off the land, the Griper at 2 A. M. of *Tuesday* the 15*th*, was able to make sail for the eastward. But we were soon re-called by signal from the Hecla, the water appearing much clearer of ice than before along shore to the westward. The Hecla, therefore, got under sail in that direction, running along not more than from 100 to 150 yards from the land, in soundings from ten to seventeen fathoms. Proceeding in this way nearly two miles to the northward of W., the ice closed in upon us so fast, that we found it impossible to make up with the Hecla, and were obliged to put in to the shore in very deep water, where, had the ice set in upon us, it would have been beyond our power to save the vessel. The Hecla, which was a considerable distance ahead, drew within a number of heavy masses of grounded ice, where she might not only be tolerably secure herself, but have it in her power to afford us assistance along shore if necessary. Captain Parry walked round to consult with our commander on the means to be adopted to save the provisions and stores, should the Griper be wrecked or abandoned, informing him of the measures recommended by the officers of the Hecla.

In the evening, a party from the Hecla returned from a hunting expedition, bringing in nine hares, for the birds had already, in a great measure, deserted us.

In the morning of the 16th, Captain Parry, with some gentlemen of the Hecla, the weather being clear, and the wind having blown for a whole day from the westward, walked for a couple of miles along the high land in that direction: but they had the mortification to find, that the ice out to sea continued entire and wholly inaccessible. The only opening visible was a narrow channel close to the shore, on to a bold point bearing N. 52° W., distant above two miles, apparently the western extremity of Melville Island, and which was, therefore, named Cape Dundas. From the inequalities of the surface of the ice, as far as could be discovered to the westward, it really resembled an extent of low land. The trending of the island to the north westward, and the uniformly compact appearance of the ice in that direction, showed that all navigation, in the course proposed, was impracticable: it was, therefore, again resolved to attempt a passage by standing farther to the southward. The station of the ships, at this time, was the farthest westward of our whole voyage, in latitude 74° 26′ 25″, and longitude, by the chronometer, 113° 46′ 44″. But Cape Dundas, the westernmost visible point of Melville Island, was in lat. 74° 27′ 50″, and long. 103° 57′ 35″. Thus, the known extent of the island must be about 135 miles, from E.N.E. to W.S.W., and the breadth north from Winter Harbour between forty and fifty miles. Getting again under sail at 2 P.M., we turned our heads to the eastward along the shore, in the hope of finding some opening to allow us to stand to the southward; but the ice closing in fast to the land, it was with no little difficulty that, about midnight, we turned a point on which were several large masses of ice aground, to which the ships were made fast. The Hecla got into a situation tolerably secure among the bergs, as we called them, in ten to twelve fathoms of water; but our ship was much more exposed. The ice now began to form near the ships in the evenings, and the sun had not power to dissolve it in the day. On the 17th our sportsmen brought on board nine hares, still mostly white, and two dozen of ptarmigans. The sorrel was now become quite insipid.

Arriving at Cape Providence on the 23d, where we had been on the 13th September last year, the ships became quite unmanageable, being inclosed among broken bodies of ice which drew more water than either of them. In this course we received shocks heavier than any we had hitherto encountered; and, at last, we made fast about three miles to the eastward of the Cape in four fathoms water, half a mile to the westward of the Hecla, which got into from eighteen to twenty feet of water, both close to the beach. In this situation, the state of the ice and the seas, and the lateness of the season being considered, it was the unanimous opinion of the officers of both ships, that to attempt to prosecute our voyage to the westward, would be only to expose both ships and ships' companies to certain detention in the midst of the ice, for another period certainly of not less duration than that passed in Winter Harbour.

On examining our stock of provisions it appeared that, even on our present reduced rate of two-thirds of the full allowance, we could not make them serve beyond the end of November of the in-coming year. Our stock of fuel could only last to the same period, even by adopting the method, injurious to the health, of having both crews on board the Hecla. The ships were, indeed, still in good order, and the officers and men nearly as healthy as when we left England. The commander of the expedition therefore applied, by letter, to all the principal officers, surgeons, &c. of the ships, requesting within six-and-thirty hours their opinions of what was best to be done. The unanimous answer was, that the first thing would be to try to get more to the southward; and, in the case that no opening in that direction should be discovered, that then they should make the best of their way to England. This resolution being adopted, we availed ourselves of a wind from the north-westward, which opened a channel along Melville Island, and at 3 P. M. of *Saturday* the 26*th*, we were off Cape Hearne, the western point of the bay of Winter Harbour. Running, therefore, eastward along the edge of the ice, and watching every opening which seemed to lead through it to the southward, but all in vain. On the 30th we came to longitude 90° off Prince Leopold's Isles, in the entrance of Prince Regent's Inlet, and keeping nearer to the south shore of Lancaster's Sound than in our outward voyage, we last night got fairly out of the sound and entered Baffin's Bay. It is intended, as I understand, to run to the southward along the western coast of this bay and of Davis's Strait: but our observations on that tract must be reserved for another occasion.

Farewell, &c. &c.

LETTER XV.

DEAR THOMAS,

At Sea, 31st October, 1820.

It was intended, I believe, to go on shore in Possession Bay, on the south side of the entrance into Lancaster's Sound, for the purpose of examining the motion of our chronometers; because the longitude of the station in that bay was formerly accurately ascertained: but the wind being fair, and the weather good, it was not judged advisable to lose the time which that operation would demand. We, therefore, ran along parallel to the coast in a south-easterly course. In the first part of our run we had the ice between us and the land; but, afterwards, it lay a considerable way out at sea, leaving a free passage, of irregular breadth, from ten to thirty miles.

On *Tuesday*, the 5*th* of last month, in the morning, we came off the deep inlet called the River Clyde, having met with the Lee, of Hull, one of the whalers, who informed us of many occurrences in England, since our departure in May last year. Among these, we learned the public calamity sustained by the country in the deaths of our venerable sovereign George III., and of his Royal Highness the Duke of Kent. The Lee had made her way across the ice in latitude 73°, more to the southward than we had done. Learning from the master of this ship that, a few days before, he had met with some Esquimaux in the River Clyde, Captain Parry thinking it might be of service to have some communication with those people, probably entire strangers to Europeans, stood into the inlet, and, at 6 P. M., observed four canoes paddling off for the ships. I should mention, that the opportunity of the Hull ship was embraced to transmit our letters to England: mine, which have been lying by me for so many months, will therefore, I trust, reach your hands some time before we can return to the Thames.

The canoes came alongside of the Hecla without any appearance of apprehension, making all the while a most prodigious noise. Agreeably to signs made very intelligibly, the canoes were taken on board, and the Esquimaux quickly mounted the ship's side. They consisted of one old man about sixty years of age, and three younger men from twenty to thirty. When fairly on board, their noise seemed, if possible, to increase; exclaiming till they were both hoarse and out of breath. This was not, however, enough to express their delight, for, to their vociferations they joined jumping about on the deck for several minutes together; the old man himself exercising his powers as much a his weakness permitted. When asked to go down to the cabin the young men seemed unwilling till they saw the old man descend without hesitation. It was remarked, by some gentlemen of the Hecla, that these poor people behaved much better than those Esquimaux who had been seen in the former voyage of 1818, on the north-east coast of Baffin's Bay. With some difficulty the old man was made to understand that it was wished to take his picture : he, in consequence, sat with tolerable patience for an hour on a stool near the fire, until the drawing was finished. Yet all this time exchanges were going on near him, by furnishing articles to his companions for their dresses, spears, &c. This trade was conducted with great honesty on the part of the Esquimaux, at the same time that they seemed to be not unacquainted with the trade. When any thing was offered to them in exchange, if they thought it not of sufficient value, they remained silent until they found that nothing more was presented, and then agreed to the barter. When any thing was accepted by them, either in exchange or as a present, they licked it twice in token of their satisfaction. When night was coming on they expressed a desire to go on shore, a boat from the ship carrying one of them who had sold his canoe : for these frail barks hold one person only. While going to shore, the canoes could beat the boat, when the Esquimaux chose to exert themselves, and would imitate the sounds of the boatmen in rowing.

Thursday, the 7th of *September*, being the day of the remarkable eclipse, which was to be central and annular across the middle of Europe, Captain Parry and Captain Sabine landed on an island near the north shore of the inlet. But the clouds did not disperse till about half after 7 A. M., when the eclipse had already begun. Soon after 8 the sun was again clouded : nor did he again appear till twenty minutes past 9, when the eclipse was found to be over.

Soon after the boat landed on the island the old Esquimaux, and one of the younger ones passed over, carrying with them some whale-bone, and dresses of seal-skin. A boat from our ship also landed, and one of the officers drew the picture of the young man; but it was no easy matter to get him to sit still for any time, so strong is their inclination to jump about when much pleased or surprised. The old one seemed very inquisitive, observing chiefly things that seemed to be useful, in preference of others that were merely curious or amusing. Thus he was soon contented with beholding his own droll figure in a looking-glass, but seemed most anxious to obtain the mallet which he saw used to open a canister of preserved meat for the dinner of the party

Being pressed to eat some of it, they took a little, evidently from complaisance, and placed the rest in their canoes. Of rum, even when diluted with water, none of them would taste. Our party having determined the situation of the island in N. lat. 70° 21′ 57″, W. long. by the chronometers 51° 28′ 33″, variation of compass 80° 59′ 17″ westerly, rowed over about two miles westward, to a low point of land, near two Esquimaux tents, or huts. The visitors showed much dexterity in launching and getting into their canoes, having first taken great care to place the old man safely in his. As soon as the boat's crew began to row, the Esquimaux began their former imitation of our *hurra, give way,* and as there was a little sea, their canoes, it was observed, could not have kept up with the boats.

When our party came in sight of the huts, the men, women, and children came out to meet them, calling out as loud as they could *pilletay,* (give me,) the only word that could be discovered in the uproar. The dogs, on the other hand, set off to the top of a hill, to avoid the strangers. The Esquimaux at this place consisted of the four men who had been on board the Hecla, and four women, one of them perhaps the wife of the old man, for she seemed of an equal age. The other women might be of about thirty, twenty-two, and eighteen years of age. The two eldest of these had infants in bags at their backs; besides whom seven children appeared from twelve to three or four years old. One of our officers offered an axe to a woman for a dog, and she went immediately with a halter of thongs, with which she brought back one of the finest of their pack. A bargain was supposed to be settled for a canoe belonging to the old woman, and the men were going to draw it down to the water; but she had been misunderstood, for she laid hold of the canoe with loud lamentations; nor would she part with it, although a larger price than before was offered for it.

In stature these Esquimaux are much below the ordinary size of human beings. The old man, although a little bent by age, measured 4 feet 11 inches; the other men from 5 feet 4 to 5 feet 6 inches. Faces round and full, complexion not very dark, teeth white, eyes small, nose broad but not flat, hair black and straight, hands and feet remarkably small. The women about 4 feet 10 or 11 inches, features regular, eyes small, black, and quick, teeth even and very white, hair deep black, spread over the shoulders. The youngest female displayed much natural reserve, probably unmarried, for she was not tattoed, as the others were. The dresses of both sexes made of seal-skin, consist of a jacket, with a hood for the head, and trowsers. The tents in which they pass the summer are chiefly supported by a pole of whalebone, fourteen feet high, set up perpendicularly, and reaching several feet above the skins which compose the covering. The length of the tent from 16 to 18 feet, and the breadth from 7 to 9 feet. The canoe purchased by Captain Parry was very nearly 17 feet long; the greatest breadth 2 feet 1½ inch. The ribs or timbers as we call them, were of whalebone, or drift-wood, and the outward covering of the skins of the wolf or the walrus. The paddle is of fir, with a blade at each end, strengthened on the edges with pieces of bone. The dogs at this place, not fewer than 50 in number, have very much the appearance of wolves, exceedingly shy and ravenous. Within some stones in a corner of each tent, was a lamp of oil and moss, over which was a stone vessel, containing a large mess of the flesh of the walrus, or sea-horse, in the midst of a quantity of thick gravy. For want of an interpreter very little could be picked up of their language; but a bear they called *nennook*, a deer *tooktook*, and a hare *ookalik*, words nearly the same with those used on the E. coast of Baffin's Bay. Showing them a drawing of the musk-ox, they pronounced the name *oomingmack*, but seemed astonished to see its figure so small.

Bidding adieu to these honest inoffensive creatures, we stood out of the inlet in the evening of the 7th, and at the same time of the 9th, the Hecla hove too, in order to give us time to come up with her off Cape Kater, in lat. 69° 12′, the N. point of a spacious inlet running in westward. The entrance is at least 15 leagues wide, and by it may perhaps be found a passage along the N. coast of America, in a situation much more accessible than that by Sir James Lancaster's Sound.

On the 13th we stood off shore to endeavour to make way through the ice; but being greatly retarded by fogs and contrary winds, besides the strength and extent of the floes, it was not until the evening of Tuesday the 26th, that we got fairly clear; and hoisting in the boats, which had been employed to track the ships, we stood on to E.S.E., and then directed our course for Old England.

On *Monday*, the 2d of this month, we had the misfortune to be separated from our excellent fellow-adventurers in the Hecla. During a severe although fair gale, our ship was obliged to ly-to. but the Hecla receiving a heavy sea, found it necessary, as we suppose, to set more sail, and was soon out of sight. We were, however, too well acquainted with the qualities of that vessel to be under any apprehensions for her fate, and hope to join company again at Lerwick in the Shetland isles, where, as I have understood, our rendezvous is appointed, in case of separation, and where, whichever ship shall first arrive, is to wait a week for the other, and then proceed for England.

P. S. *Wednesday*, 1st November, we are at last all safe in Lerwick bay, in Shetland; but no tidings of the Hecla. She may however, knowing the trim of our vessel, have kept out to sea, n the hope of again falling in with us. At any rate we shall wait the appointed time for her appearance, and then turn our heads to the southward. This is probably, therefore the last letter which you can have from me before I have the happiness to see our excellent mother, Mary, and you, all well and comfortable in London. The occurrences of our run from Davis's Strait to these, the most northern of the Britannic Isles, in which was nothing remarkable, must, therefore, be reserved for verbal communication.

Farewell,
&c. &c.

EDITOR'S POSTSCRIPT.

THE discovery of a communication between the Atlantic and the Pacific Oceans, to the northward of the American continent, has been long an object of curiosity and enterprise. When the New World beyond the Atlantic was made known to Europeans, by the expedition of Columbus; when by the fortunate passage of Magellan through the dangerous strait of his name, it was seen that a communication existed towards the southern extremity of the new continent; that a corresponding communication also existed towards its northern extremity, it was very reasonable to conclude. Access to the treasures of India and China by the southern parts of the globe, was discovered and appropriated by Spain and Portugal. Similar access by the northern parts seemed naturally to belong to the British and other northern nations of Europe.

Such a passage by the North American coast was asserted to have been effected by Cortereal, a Portuguese, in 1500. Having visited Newfoundland, he passed over to the continent on the north of the great river St. Laurence, where, observing the country fitted for agriculture, he called it *Terra de Labrador*. Coasting still farther northward, he came to a spacious inlet running westward, and concluded he had discovered the passage so much desired. This strait he named that of Anian, probably because he conceived it to be the eastern opening of the strait so called, of which the western opening into the Pacific already bore that name. Returning full of hopes to Portugal, Cortereal was sent out the next season, to prosecute his discovery. No accounts of him being received, his brother went after him; but neither of the brothers were ever more heard of. Many years afterwards, viz. in 1576, Martin Frobisher attempted to pass to China round the northern coasts of America. He left England in July with two small vessels and a pinnace, the largest only 25 tons, and proceeding to what he supposed was a strait in N. lat. 63° 10', he returned to England in the beginning of October. On a second voyage he arrived on the west coast of Greenland, and brought home certain sparkling stones, supposed to contain gold. Frobisher's third voyage, with many ships and a number of colonists, was defeated by the ice, and he returned once more unsuccessful.

In 1585 a fresh attempt to discover the North-west passage was made by a number of noblemen and gentlemen of England, who dispatched John Davis, a Devonshire-man, on the pursuit. On the 20th July he came on the southern point of Greenland, which he very naturally named Cape Desolation. In this voyage, and in a second of the following year, he never reached beyond lat. 66° 40'; but in his third, in 1587, he penetrated through the strait now known by his name, as far as lat. 72° 12'. Then directing his course westward, his people were alarmed at the ice, and he returned to England in September.

The failures of Davis did not quite discourage other adventurers in the north-west expedition; but none of them had any success. At last Capt. Henry Hudson, a skilful and intrepid seaman, who had before endeavoured to penetrate to China along the north of Europe and Asia, was in 1610 sent out by a company of English merchants, to make his way by the north of America. Penetrating by the strait now known by his name, he entered the great bay, and standing southwards to the bottom, where he purposed to collect game and other provisions, and pass the winter, in order to prosecute his researches at the first favourable season, his people mutinied, and turned the unfortunate Hudson, with his son and five other persons, adrift in a boat, amidst the ice, where he no doubt soon perished. Two years afterwards, in 1612, Sir Thomas Button undertook the search for a north-west passage. Passing through Hudson's Strait he came on the continent of America, in N. lat. 60° 40'. He wintered in Port Nelson, so called from his pilot, in lat. 57° 40', now the principal station of the Hudson's Bay Company. In 1616, Baffin and Bylot reached northwards through Davis's Strait, and the bay named after Baffin, as far as N. lat. 78°. Then turning down by the west coast, they passed Alderman Jones's Sound, and opened Sir James Lancaster's Sound, and returned to England.

In 1741, Captain Middleton, of the navy, was sent out to pursue the search. He entered Hudson's Strait and stood to the northward, into what he termed Repulse Bay, because there he stated himself to be quite shut in by land on the north and west. The account he gave of his expedition was very unsatisfactory to the Admiralty; and, in consequence, by their suggestion, an Act of Parliament passed in 1743 (18 Geo. II.), granting a reward of 20,000l. to any British subject who should discover the north-west passage.

Besides these and other real expeditions, in the year 1708 in London appeared an account of a voyage stated to have been performed in 1640, by Fuenta, or De Fonte, by the north-west passage. But that work is now considered merely as a romance, in which some facts, collected from other voyages, are interspersed in a mass of fiction. The whole is disavowed by the Spanish writers.

Very lately an account has appeared of another voyage, said to have been accomplished in 1588, by a Spanish Captain, Laurence-Ferrer Maldonado, from the coast of Labrador, or the Esquimaux country on the north of the River St. Laurence to the Pacific Ocean. The original MS. of this voyage is said to be preserved among the papers of a Spanish nobleman of the first rank. In examining the MSS. in the Ambrosian Library, in Milan, one was discovered of Maldonado's voyage, and lately published in Italian. It contains, however, so many errors in geographical science, that it seems best, in the present state of our knowledge of the original work, to suspend all judgement respecting its authenticity.

The letters contained in the preceding pages come no lower down than the 1st *November*, when the Griper arrived in Lerwick or Brassa Bay, in Shetland. It is necessary, however, to add, that the Hecla having suffered very severely in a gale of wind, before she came near those islands, was obliged to make all way for Leith, where she arrived, for the purpose of repair, on the 3d of *November*. Captain Parry landing at Peterhead, reached London in the morning of the same day. Both ships entered the Thames in the middle of that month, and were paid off at Deptford, on the 21st of *December*, 1820.

THE END.

For EU product safety concerns, contact us at Calle de José Abascal, 56–1º,
28003 Madrid, Spain or eugpsr@cambridge.org.

www.ingramcontent.com/pod-product-compliance
Ingram Content Group UK Ltd.
Pitfield, Milton Keynes, MK11 3LW, UK
UKHW041419180426
11947UKWH00007B/211